Álvar Núñez Cabeza de Vaca

The Great Pedestrian
of North and South America

Borald E. Chipman

By Donald E. Chipman

Texas State Historical Association
Denton

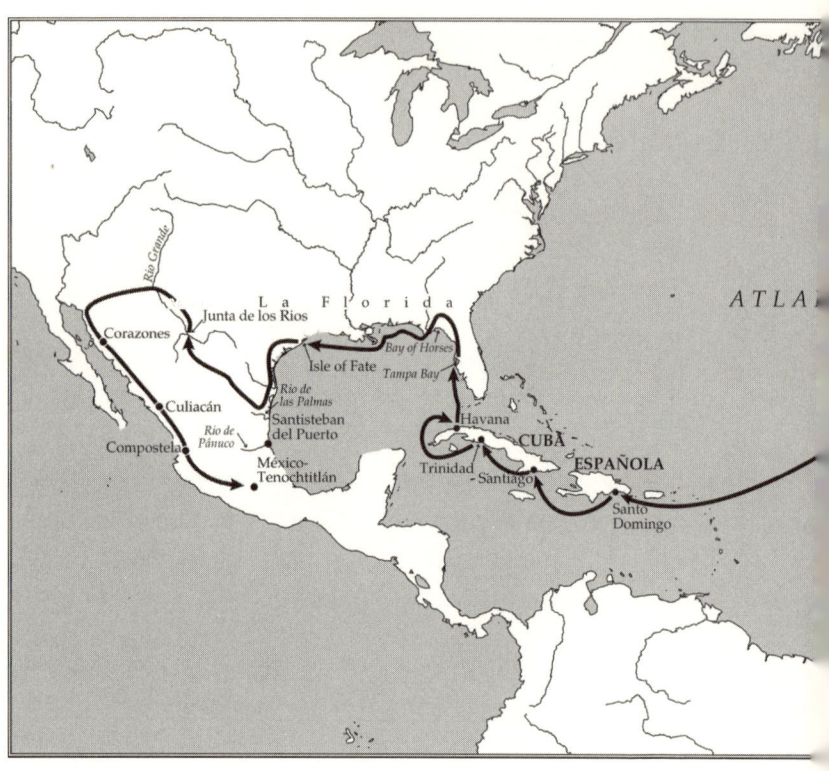

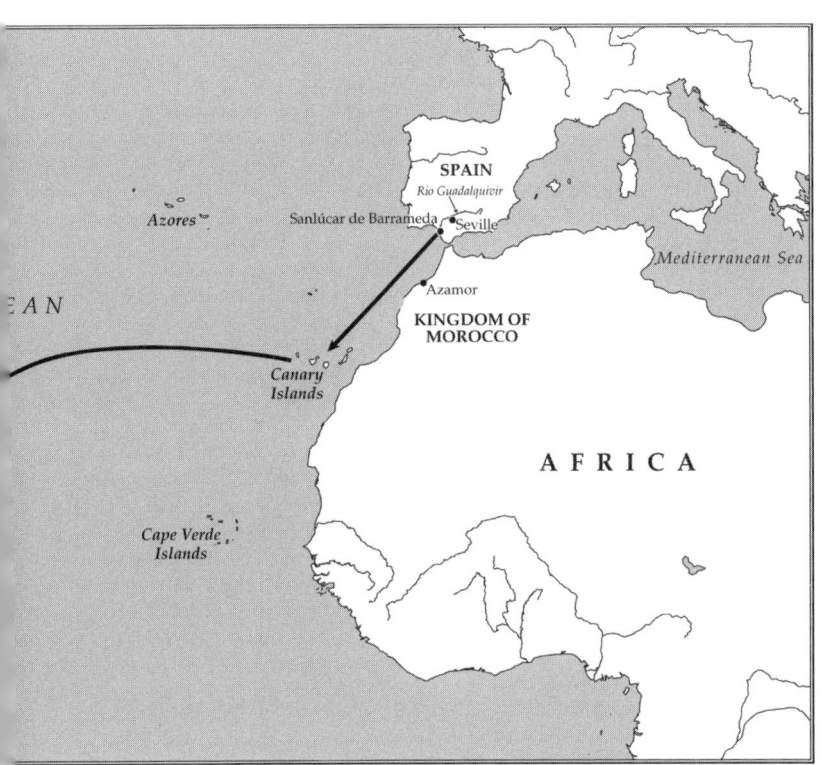

Azores

Sanlúcar de Barrameda

SPAIN
Rio Guadalquivir
Seville

Mediterranean Sea

Azamor

KINGDOM OF
MOROCCO

Canary
Islands

Cape Verde
Islands

A F R I C A

:AN

© 2012 by the Texas State Historical Association
All rights reserved. Printed in the U.S.A.
Number twenty in the Fred Rider Cotten Popular History Series

Library of Congress Cataloging-in-Publication Data

Chipman, Donald E.
Álvar Núñez Cabeza de Vaca : the great pedestrian / by Donald E. Chipman.
(Fred Rider Cotten popular history series; no. 20)
    Includes bibliographical references.
    ISBN 978-0-87611-251-9
    1. Núñez Cabeza de Vaca, Álvar, 16th cent. 2. Explorers—America—Biography. 3. Explorers—Spain—Biography. 4. America—Discovery and exploration—Spanish. I. Title. II. Series: Fred Rider Cotten popular history series; no. 20.

Published by the Texas State Historical Association

Frontispiece: Cabeza de Vaca's travels from Spain and throughout North America. Cartography by Mapping Specialists, Fitchburg, Wisconsin. Courtesy Andrés Résendez.

CONTENTS

ACKNOWLEDGEMENTS

I WISH TO THANK those who helped me prepare this book as well as improve its accuracy and readability. Foremost in importance are two individuals: Ryan R. Schumacher, Associate Editor of the *Southwestern Historical Quarterly* and my editor at the Texas State Historical Association (TSHA) in Denton, Texas; and Robert S. Weddle of Bonham, Texas, independent scholar and historian extraordinary, who critiqued the manuscript for the TSHA Press and recommended its publication as a Cotten Book. The book also profited from a careful reading and helpful suggestions offered by Randolph B. "Mike" Campbell, Chief Historian of the TSHA and Editor of the *Southwestern Historical Quarterly* as well as from readings and critiques by Doris I. Chipman in Denton, Texas. I especially wish to thank Richard B. McCaslin, Chair of the Department of History at the University of North Texas, for underwriting the cost of permissions and cartography for this volume.

Two historians with books on Cabeza de Vaca, David A. Howard and Andrés Reséndez, generously agreed to my use of maps appearing in their works. The University of Alabama Press (UAP), which published Howard's *Conquistador in Chains* (1997) and holds the copyright on it, granted formal permission for map reproduction, and I wish to thank Claire Lewis Evans, Digital Projects & Rights and Permissions, at UAP for extending that courtesy. Andrés Reséndez owns the copyright of six maps appearing in his book but gave me permission to reproduce them in publishable format by Don Larson, Project Manager, at Mapping Specialists, Ltd., in Fitchburg, Wisconsin.

Additional thanks are extended to John Overholt, Assistant Curator at the Houghton Library, Harvard University, for obtaining a digital reproduction of Cabeza de Vaca's coat of arms in a rare book by Joseph Pellicer de Tovar (Madrid, 1652), and for granting me permission to use it as an illustration; to Don Carleton, Executive Director of The University of Texas Dolph Briscoe Center for American History (DBCAH) for permission to reproduce the cover of Cabeza de Vaca's 1555 edition of his *Relación,* housed at the DBCAH—as well as to Alexander Mendoza, Assistant Professor of History at the University of North Texas, for his help with cartography.

INTRODUCTION

CABEZA DE VACA'S mode of transportation, afoot on portions of two continents in the early decades of the sixteenth century, fits one dictionary definition of the word "pedestrian." By no means, however, should the related meanings of "commonplace" or "prosaic" be applied to the man or his remarkable adventures. Between 1528 and 1536, he trekked across an estimated 2,480 to 2,640 miles of North American terrain from the Texas coast, near Galveston Island, to San Miguel de Culiacán, near the Pacific Coast of Mexico.[1] He then traveled under better circumstances, although still on foot, to Mexico City, where he arrived in late July 1536. About a year later, Cabeza de Vaca returned to Spain, where he sought appointment as governor of lands he had explored, only to learn that the position he thought rightfully to be his had been awarded to Hernando de Soto. As a consolation prize, the king in 1540 granted Cabeza de Vaca civil and military authority over a region centered in modern-day Asunción, Paraguay, but in total extending from the Río de la Plata estuary on the north to Tierra del Fuego on the south. Its western limits were the Andes Mountains and the jurisdiction of Chile.

After a dangerous Atlantic crossing, Cabeza de Vaca landed near the Brazilian coast on Santa Catalina Island in March 1541 at the onset of winter in the Southern Hemisphere.[2] In the following October when the spring season had begun, Cabeza de Vaca led some 250 soldiers and colonists, including a few married women and two friars, on an overland journey of four and a half months' duration that covered approximately 1,200 miles from the coast of Brazil to the Spanish outpost at Asunción.[3] Although the expedition contained twenty-six horses, Cabeza de Vaca chose to impress his command by taking off his shoes and walking barefoot every step of the way! He was the first European to see and describe Iguazú Falls, by volume the largest cataracts in the world.[4] By some accounts, his expedition suffered no loss of lives. Others state that one man fell victim to a jungle cat, and a second either drowned in a river or died from an Indian arrow—in any case, a remarkable record of leadership.

Cabeza de Vaca's life from birth between the years 1487 to 1492 to his death c. 1559, and his extraordinary interludes of travel and adventure on two American continents unfolds in the following pages. Therein, the reader will encounter his amazing story—perhaps without parallel—in the annals of Spain in the New World.

Chapter 1

By HIS NAME ALONE, Cabeza de Vaca (Cow's Head) stirs interest among readers of all ages. The oft-repeated explanation of his surname's origin, dating from the battle of Las Navas de Tolosa in 1212 during the Spanish Reconquest (c. 720–1492), started with accounts of a mythical ancestor of Cabeza de Vaca, a shepherd named Martín de Alhaja, who supposedly marked a pass in the Sierra Morena of central Spain with a cow's skull that allowed Christian forces to flank and defeat a Muslim army. Without question, the story is apocryphal.[5]

In 1999 the University of Nebraska Press published three massive volumes, each more than four hundred pages in length, on Cabeza de Vaca. The authors, Rolena Adorno and Patrick Charles Pautz, refute the legend of Martín de Alhaja's heroics in a most convincing manner by tracing the ancestry of Cabeza de Vaca through sixteen generations. In doing so, they arrive at the year 1200, twelve years *prior to* the battle of Las Navas de Tolosa. In that year, the first on record to bear the name Cabeza de Vaca was Inés Pérez Cabeza de Vaca, the wife of Rodrigo Rodríguez Girón and Cabeza de Vaca's grandmother many times removed.[6] Unfortunately, Adorno and Pautz have no explanation for the surname's origin but do note that the common Spanish family name of Baca is the equivalent of Vaca.

Cabeza de Vaca's birth year cannot be determined from extant sources. This, however, is far from unusual. Spaniards testifying as witnesses in literally thousands of lawsuits spawned by some of the most litigious people ever to draw a breath were invariably asked to state their name and age as part of the swearing-in process. With rare exceptions, witnesses when addressing their age would say, for example: *treinta y cinco años, poco más o menos* (thirty-five years, a little more or less).

Adorno and Pautz could only arrive at a "birth window" for Cabeza de Vaca, the years 1487–1492.[7] His place of birth can be identified as Jerez de la Frontera in the south of Spain, a region renowned for its amber-colored wine known as sherry—the name being a corruption of Jerez. Thanks to Adorno and Pautz, the parentage of Cabeza de Vaca can, of course, be likewise ascertained with certainty through fifteen generations prior to his, but concern here is limited to his paternal grandfather, parents, and maternal ancestors.

Pedro de Vera, Cabeza de Vaca's paternal grandfather, was a man of notable accomplishments. A contemporary Castilian writer described him as "a nobleman, expert in battles on land and on the sea." And, indeed, his signal services for the Catholic Monarchs, Ferdinand and Isabella, were as conqueror and military governor of the island of Gran Canaria in the 1480s, followed by his role as purveyor and supplier of goods for the Spanish army in the war of Granada, which concluded the nearly eight-hundred-year Reconquest on January 2, 1492.[8] Despite his loyal service to the Catholic Monarchs, Pedro de Vera was not remunerated and died poor, leaving no estate to his heirs.

Cabeza de Vaca's father, Francisco de Vera, had a far less illustrious career than don Pedro. He saw military action in the war of Granada and served as councilman of the city of Jerez de la Frontera from roughly 1482 to 1503. He was deceased by 1506 and interred in the monastery of Santo Domingo in Jerez de la Frontera, a family burial site obtained by Pedro de Vera.[9]

Doña Teresa Cabeza de Vaca, don Álvar's mother, was the daughter of Pedro Fernández Cabeza de Vaca and his second wife, Catalina de Zurita y Figueroa.[10] It was doña Teresa's surname, Cabeza de Vaca, that was proudly adopted by her son, Álvar, rather than that of Vera from his father. Adopting a maternal surname was far from unique, as those familiar with Hispanic family name preferences can attest. In fact, even name variations among full bloodline siblings could vary greatly in these early times. For example, Nuño Beltrán de Guzmán, a Spanish official and important contemporary of Cabeza de Vaca, had a brother named Gómez Suárez de Figueroa. Without research of Guzmán family history, identifying the close relationship of these two men with such variant names would be difficult.

In 1509 Cabeza de Vaca's mother followed her husband in death, leaving Álvar and his two younger brothers homeless. Pedro de Vera, a distant relative, was then named trustee and guardian of the children of Francisco de Vera and Teresa Cabeza de Vaca.[11] But at this time, young Álvar had already entered ducal service around 1503 as a page in the house of the Dukes of Medina Sidonia in Andalusia.

Given the military prowess of Cabeza de Vaca's paternal grandfather in Gran Canaria and the War of Granada, as well as his father's service in the latter campaign, it is not surprising that young Álvar would be at-tracted to the profession of arms. In 1511 he left ducal service for roughly two years while serving in the Spanish army. He saw active duty in Italy and fought at the battle of Ravenna in 1512.[12] His vivid recollections of the violence and continuous warfare of late-Renaissance Italy left a lasting impression on him. Much later, while living among Indians in Texas, he would liken some of them in cunningness and viciousness to the Italians.

After returning to ducal service in 1513, a position he held until 1527, Cabeza de Vaca married María Marmolejo around 1520.[13] The couple would remain married, even during the long years of separation from the late 1520s to the mid-1530s when don Álvar was presumed dead in the wilds of European-unexplored North America. If Cabeza de Vaca can be viewed as having survived odysseys in the New World as a sort of "Span-ish Odysseus," then María Marmolejo, although she did not have to wait twenty years for his return, surely qualifies as a "Spanish Penelope."

As it turned out, it was Cabeza de Vaca's marriage that largely influ-enced his return to combat in 1520, with important implications for him well beyond that year. His wife was a *converso*, meaning a member of a Jewish family who converted to Christianity after the enforced royal edicts of 1492. These draconian laws issued on March 30 compelled all Jews in Spain to either convert to Christianity or leave the country after four months. The powerful Dukes of Medina Sidonia had an admirable record of protecting conversos in Andalusia from persecution as apostate Chris-tians. But a civil war in Spain, known as the Revolt of the Comuneros (May 1520–April 1521), broke out around the time of don Álvar and doña María's nuptials. Should the rebel Comuneros prevail over forces loyal to young Charles I, who had ascended the Spanish throne in 1516, it threat-ened the safety of doña María and other conversos in Andalusia.[14]

The Revolt of the Comuneros is far too complex to analyze in depth in a brief treatment of Cabeza de Vaca. It is important to note that it sprang from the immense unpopularity of the foreign-born, non-Span-ish-speaking king Charles I, the son of Juana la Loca and her feckless and unfaithful Hapsburg husband, Philip the Handsome. Young Charles grew up in Flanders, spoke Flemish, and had never set foot in Spain until he succeeded his grandfather, the Catholic Monarch Ferdinand, as a teenage king. Accompanying the new monarch to Spain were rapacious Burgun-dian and Flemish advisers who looted Spanish coffers, pushed aside old-family nobles at court, and treated all Spaniards with contempt. Hatreds that simmered for more than three years erupted into civil war when Charles left the country in May 1520, en route to his crowning as the Holy Roman Emperor Charles V.[15]

The Revolt of the Comuneros ended after slightly less than a year of fighting that resulted in total victory for royalist forces that rallied on behalf of the absent king. A cursory analysis of a few prominent families who fought in support of King Charles suggests that this revolt and its suppression served as an important litmus test of loyalty for men soon chosen for service across thousands of miles of ocean in the Americas. Among staunch adherents of the king were the family Mendoza, whose members would serve as viceroys of New Spain (Colonial Mexico) and Peru and first governor of La Plata; the family Velasco, both father and son, who would head the Viceroyalty of New Spain on three occasions; the family Guzmán, from whom came a man who controlled the government in Mexico City in the late 1520s and received appointment as governor of two provinces; and, finally, the family Cabeza de Vaca, represented by don Álvar, who in 1527 would be appointed royal treasurer and second in command of the Pánfilo de Narváez expedition.

The Narváez expedition was charged with exploring and settling what was then known as "Florida"—at that time regarded as an immense expanse of land extending along the Gulf Coast from the Florida peninsula to the Río de las Palmas, today the Río Soto la Marina in the present state of Tamaulipas in northeast Mexico. This expedition merits detailed attention, for reasons that are central to the story of Cabeza de Vaca's first assignment and adventure in the Americas. And it cannot be understood without the context of Hernando Cortés's conquest of Mexico from Spanish island possessions in the Caribbean.

The island known to Spaniards as Española (the Dominican Republic and Haiti of today) was permanently settled by Christopher Columbus in 1493. By 1508 Puerto Rico and Jamaica had fallen under the control of Juan Ponce de León and Juan de Esquivel, respectively. Then in 1511, Diego de Velázquez initiated the conquest of Cuba, the largest island in the Antillean chain. From Puerto Rico, León first landed in Florida in 1513, formally opening the history of Spain on the North American continent. From Cuba, Velázquez later sponsored the sea expeditions of Francisco Hernández de Córdoba (1517) and Juan de Grijalva (1518), which made landfall on the Yucatán peninsula, where they acquired some wealth but clashed with Maya Indians.[16]

Governor Velázquez's choice as commander of a third expedition fell to Hernando Cortés, who had served him as secretary in the conquest of Cuba. As preparations neared completion, Cortés began to display an alarming independence—in part, because it was don Hernando's nature to be a leader, and because Cortés himself was a minority investor in the enterprise. But as the final hours of preparations neared, Velázquez became convinced that he could not count on the loyalty of such a headstrong captain, and he attempted to remove Cortés from command. The governor's decision, however, came too late. Cortés rallied his men and left Cuba before Velázquez could replace him with a more compliant captain.[17] Significantly, when Cortés left Cuba in 1519 he was viewed as a renegade conquistador by his enraged former sponsor. It also meant that Velázquez would spare no effort or expense in his attempts to remove Cortés from command—all vitally important to the life and fortunes of Cabeza de Vaca, whose American exploits were nonetheless still some eight years in the future.

The conquest of Mexico by Hernando Cortés is too well known to recount here beyond details important to this book. From the coast of Mexico, Cortés marched inland and gained allies along the way among Indian groups, especially the Tlaxcalans, who had suffered from wars fought with the powerful Aztecs. The Spanish captain occupied the Aztec capital of Tenochtitlan in 1519 without firing a shot and later took hostage Moctezuma II.

By 1520 Cortés was in control of much of Mexico from the Veracruz settlement to the Aztec capital, and he had founded the town of Segura de la Frontera on the road from Tlaxcala to Veracruz. But in April a sizable Velázquez-sponsored expedition led by Pánfilo de Narváez landed on the coast of Mexico with orders from the governor of Cuba to arrest Cortés and remove him from command. Approximately one thousand foot soldiers and eighty horses made up the army led by Narváez, which outnumbered Cortés's forces by a margin of roughly four to one.[18]

When news reached Cortés of the Velázquez-Narváez challenge to his command, he responded in a manner consistent with his bent for leadership. He first tried a negotiated settlement with Narváez, which came to naught because of don Pánfilo's conviction that he held the whip hand due to superior numbers. Cortés then divided his small army that occupied the Aztec capital, leaving about eighty men there, while he force-marched a larger contingent of troops numbering around 270 to the coast. En route he received small reinforcements from his adherents at Segura de la Frontera. Under cover of darkness, Cortes's much smaller but more experienced army quickly routed Narváez's forces. In fighting on the steps of a pyramid in the Indian town of Cempoala, Narváez wielded a great two-handed sword, but in the darkness he did little damage with it. One of Cortés's soldiers managed to thrust a pike inside the deadly arc of the broadsword. It struck Narváez in the face and plucked out his right eye. This took the fight out of don Pánfilo, and the rest of his army quickly surrendered.[19] The outcome, however, underscores an important interpretive point—the sharp contrast between the red-bearded Narváez's ineptness and the excellent leadership of Cortés.

Cortés placed Narváez in chains and incarcerated him in humid and mosquito-infested Veracruz where he remained until 1522, at which time or perhaps a bit later he left New Spain for Cuba. But the one-eyed casualty of Cempoala did not return to Spain until 1525, still chafing over his treatment by Cortés and seeking vindication before Charles V and his court. In the meantime, he had had to stomach news of Cortés's having received an array of titles in October 1522, including the right to expel from New Spain persons whose presence he deemed prejudicial to the best interests of the king. That Velázquez's investments in the conquest of Mexico had gone unrecognized and unrewarded by the Spanish crown sent a clear message that it valued success above all other considerations.[20] For Narváez, there was no consolation from the crown until December 1526 when he received approval for the governorship of Florida and the Río de las Palmas.[21]

For approximately two years, Narváez had followed the court of Charles V as it moved about Spain, during which time his entreaties for an appointment in the New World shrewdly played on the young king's conscience. Surely, Narváez argued, delays in granting him a license to carry out an expedition in the New World would prey on Charles's mind "if it hindered the conversion of the Indians to our holy Catholic faith and postponed the benefits of your royal patrimony."[22]

Cabeza de Vaca's appointment as royal treasurer and second in command in the Narváez expedition came in mid-February 1527. It would seem that his service in the Spanish army and especially his support of Charles I in the Revolt of the Comuneros helped secure these honors for him. His annual salary of 130,000 maravedís, the smallest coin and unit of Spanish currency, was roughly half that accorded don Pánfilo. However, whereas Narváez received a guaranteed annual income of 250,000 maravedís for the rest of his life, Cabeza de Vaca's stipend was payable only for the duration of his appointment.[23]

With his royal charter in hand, Pánfilo de Narváez traveled to Seville, where he plunged into the details of organizing his expedition over the course of some six months. He needed recruits, supplies, and ships, and above all a pilot knowledgeable of coastal Florida. Such pilots, licensed by the Spanish House of Trade, were always in great demand for expeditions headed to the Indies, as Spain named its American empire. By late spring 1527, Narváez had purchased five ships and signed on approximately six hundred passengers.[24] Among those adventurers were four men whom fate would bond in a distant land that was Texas. Their names were

Alonso del Castillo, Andrés Dorantes, a Moroccan-born slave known only by the name of Estevanico, and, of course, Álvar Núñez Cabeza de Vaca. Overall, the other passengers, as historian Andrés Reséndez has remarked, were neither cardboard figures nor "gold-crazed conquistadors madly brandishing their swords, but rather ordinary men and women with their own struggles and fears and dreams." All bound for the Indies, even slaves, were at least nominal Roman Catholics, and it is unlikely that most of those who professed that faith were recent converts, so-called New Christians who were former Jews and Muslims. Some of the throng had previously been in the Indies, a few were Portuguese and Greeks, and still others were married couples.[25] What all of them most likely sought was the opportunity for a new life in a New World.

The Narváez expedition departed from Sanlúcar de Barrameda, at the mouth of the Guadalquivir River, on June 17, 1527. Some thirty-five years had passed since the Columbian voyages of the early 1490s, and travel across the Atlantic to the Caribbean islands and beyond to North American ports, although always dangerous, was not especially noteworthy to those who wrote about the early years of Spain in the Americas. So this Atlantic crossing occasioned little comment from Cabeza de Vaca, nor was it described by Spanish chroniclers. However, Spanish voyages to the Indies typically included a stopover in the Canary Islands for ship repairs and re-provisioning of food and drink. After leaving the Canaries, it would appear from comments made by Cabeza de Vaca that the Atlantic crossing took about forty-five days.[26]

The expedition apparently spent August and September on Española before moving on to Cuba, an island well familiar to Narváez. At both islands there was an urgent need to acquire horses—scarce and expensive mounts but much more preferable to having to transport them across the Atlantic. By fall, with plans still in place for continuing in that season to Florida and the Río de las Palmas, the expedition had lost approximately 140 men who, according to Cabeza de Vaca, had chosen to stay on Española to take advantage of "the favors and promises that the men of that land made to them."[27]

Unfortunately for the Narváez expedition, its island stopovers in September and October had come at the height of the hurricane season, with impending consequences. From Santiago, Cuba, the main settlement on the eastern side of the island, Narváez placed Cabeza de Vaca in command of two ships that sailed some 280 miles west to the town of Trinidad, where Narváez had been promised victuals. The vessels had barely made port, about three miles from the town, when the weather turned bad, accompanied by squalls and pounding surf. While Cabeza de

Vaca stayed with the ships, a landing party of thirty men traveled to the town to obtain the much-needed supplies. Two days later, with the weather steadily worsening, Cabeza de Vaca's presence in Trinidad was urgently requested, and although reluctant to leave the ships, he traveled there on horseback, whereupon the full brunt of a hurricane hit.[28]

In the words of Cabeza de Vaca, "At this time the sea and the storm began to swell so much that there was no less tempest in the town than at sea, because all the houses and churches blew down, and it was necessary for us to band together in groups of seven or eight, our arms locked with one another, in order to save ourselves from being carried away by the wind. We were as fearful of being killed by walking under trees as among the houses, since the storm was so great that even the trees, like the houses, fell. In this great storm and continual danger we walked all night without finding an area or place where we could be safe for even half an hour."[29]

On the following day, Cabeza de Vaca and about thirty companions who had stayed at the town of Trinidad began looking for the two ships, only to learn that the vessels were lost, and that all sixty men and twenty horses on board had perished. The winds had been so strong that they discovered a rowboat from one of the ships on top of some trees about three-quarters of a mile from shore.[30]

The surviving Spaniards suffered for several days in this hurricane-devastated region of Cuba that had been stripped of food and resources. Indeed, the storm's intensity had denuded all leaves from the trees and grass from the land. On November 5, four ships under the command of Narváez arrived at anchorage and rescued the Cabeza de Vaca party. But the hurricane and its aftermath had put an end to all plans for an autumn landing in Florida and the Río de las Palmas.[31]

Cabeza de Vaca temporarily took charge of the four remaining ships and their passengers at the port of Jagua in the Bay of Cienfuegos on the south coast of Cuba. This was winter headquarters for the expedition until mid-February 1528. During the early stay at Jagua, Narváez resumed command when he returned there with a fifth ship, a two-masted brigantine, and an experienced pilot named Miruelo who claimed to have been to the region of the Río de las Palmas.[32] The pilot's assertion may well have been true, but nonetheless had acquired very little notion of Gulf ports.

The Narváez expedition, then consisting of five ships, traveled from Cuba to the west of Florida, starting in late February or early March and ending on April 15, 1528. Land had been sighted on April 12, but the sea voyage had resulted in a great deal of disorientation, and the pilot Miruelo

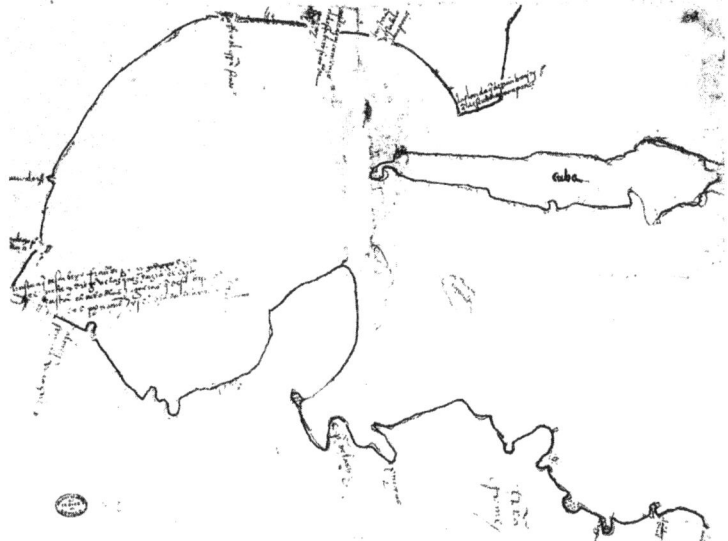

Figure 1. Sketch map of the Gulf of Mexico drawn by pilots of the Alonso Álvarez de Pineda expedition of 1519. Permission by the Archivo General de Indias, Seville, Spain; Mapas y Planos, México 5.

was unfamiliar with coastal Florida. From anchorage near Tampa Bay, Miruelo declared the Río de las Palmas to be no more than thirty to forty-five miles away, when the actual distance via the coast was more than 1,500 miles![33] It is also curious that Miruelo, who seems to have been to the east coast of Mexico in the early 1520s, would not have seen the anomaly of the sun rising over land at Florida rather than Gulf waters. Like some in positions of leadership, Miruelo apparently could not admit that he was confused or mistaken.

Miruelo's gross miscalculation of the distance by land to the Río de las Palmas also illustrates the lack of cumulative geographic and cartographic knowledge that could have come from Spaniards who had already discovered new lands or sailed unfamiliar waters in the Indies. For example, by 1528, when Narváez and company landed on the west coast of Florida, the Gulf Coast from Yucatán to about half of the Florida peninsula had been explored and sketch mapped by 1519 (see Figure 1). Later, in the early 1520s, there had been brief settlement on the Río Pánuco, inland from modern-day Tampico—followed soon after, by exploration of the much-sought Río de las Palmas, about ninety miles north of the Pánuco. In 1523 Cortés had founded the town of Santiesteban del

Puerto on the right bank of the Río Pánuco, and by May 1527 the province of Pánuco had been placed under the governorship of Nuño de Guzmán.[34] However, since it was customary for all early discovery and settlement ventures in the Indies to be privately financed, information resulting thereof was jealously guarded. Worse, it would be many decades later before the Spanish crown would demand that its subjects submit copies of maps or geographic information on new lands for systematic filing and information dissemination. Had this happened earlier, there would have been no logical reason for the Narváez expeditionaries to look for a river in Florida, which was known by other Spaniards to be far westward. Lacking basic cartographic information of the Gulf Coast, Pánfilo de Narváez would separate about three hundred men from their support vessels and land them on the Florida coast near Tampa Bay on April 15, 1528. Of that number, less than 1½ percent would live long enough to reach Spanish-settled regions of New Spain.

CHAPTER 2

NARVÁEZ AND HIS COMPANY of three hundred men apparently landed just south of Tampa Bay. Unfortunately, during the long and storm-tossed voyage from Cuba, about half of the eighty horses had died or suffered broken legs and were thrown overboard. The men were advantaged by arriving on shore in rowboats, whereas the weakened horses were lowered into the water by booms and slings and forced to swim a short distance (see Figure 2). Nearby Indians who observed the arrival of these strange men and their animals wisely chose to flee, abandoning their dwellings. In rummaging through the Indians' belongings, the Spaniards found mostly fish nets but also one rattle made of gold, which seemed to augur well for the adventurers.[35]

Narváez claimed the land for the king and himself, and on the second day, according to Cabeza de Vaca: "The governor raised the standard on Your Majesty's behalf and took possession of the land in Your royal name and was obeyed as governor just as Your Majesty commanded." Cabeza de Vaca also noted that forty-two horses had made it ashore but lamented that "these few that remained were so thin and worn out that for the present we could make little use of them."[36]

From a base on the Florida coast, the expeditionaries spent the next two weeks exploring their surroundings, while the ships remained at anchorage. One group marched north and soon had to skirt a very large inland body of water, most likely Tampa Bay, before returning to camp. This reconnaissance then prompted a large party of Spaniards to march around the bay. A few miles to the north of it, the men made a disturbing discovery. Indians there had in their possession several Castilian-made wooden crates, each containing the body of a Spaniard covered in painted deer skins—the obvious remains of a shipwrecked crew. Narváez's men also found other items of European manufacture such as shoes, linen cloth, and iron products.[37]

Figure 2. Method of loading, unloading, and transporting horses in the sixteenth century. After Manuel Ossorio y Vega, *Manera real en que se propone lo que deben saber los cavalleros* (Madrid, 1760).

To fray Juan Suárez, bishop designate of Florida and the Río de las Palmas, the crated bodies represented devil-inspired idolatry, and he ordered them burned. As historian Andrés Reséndez has remarked of the Spaniards, "these outsiders had become downright abusive."[38] These same strangers would at their peril continue this pattern of behavior toward Indians.

Natives of the bay area, anxious to be rid of unwelcome visitors, possessed a few gold ornaments that quickly piqued Spanish interests. When asked the origin of these precious objects, the natives mentioned a province very far from where they lived called Apalachee. There gold could be found in abundance.[39] This apparent ruse to rid themselves of European interlopers was used by many Indians in the Americas, and it often fell on eager ears. It seems likely that the first words of Spanish learned by many Indians were "*más allá.*" "Farther on," Spaniards were told, they would find legendary wealth but at the same time Indians hoped they would be lured to a land that would permanently swallow them.

Throughout the sixteenth century, and even into the early years of the following century, Spaniards who came to the New World saw it "through medieval spectacles." Some of them were influenced by St. Augustine who had devoted a chapter of *The City of God* to the question of whether descendants of Adam and Noah had produced monstrous and bizarre offspring. All of them remembered the façades of medieval churches that sprouted griffins, gargoyles, and a mixture of man and beast. So, beyond every mountain and distant horizon, Spanish captains looked for mythical and fabulous creatures, such as Amazon women, giants, white-haired boys, bearded ladies, headless folk with an eye in their navel, and trumpet-blowing apes. They also hoped to find Eldorado, where gold was so plentiful that Indians paved streets with it. Still another legend that died slowly for Spaniards was the hope of finding the Seven Cities of Cíbola, wealthy settlements supposedly established in a distant land across the Ocean Sea by seven Catholic bishops who had fled the Iberian Peninsula during the Muslim conquest. This prospect in particular lent credence in the aftermath of the Narváez expedition, as it had previously found impetus following the defeat of the powerful and rich Aztec Empire by Cortés in 1521.[40]

This chimera vision likely prompted Pánfilo de Narváez to make, as it turned out, his worst decision as captain of the expedition: "All able bodied men and horses would proceed on foot, going inland at times but keeping parallel to the coast until they reached the Río de las Palmas"— again, believed to be no more than forty-five miles up the coast (see Figure 3). There were dissenters to this plan, among whom was Cabeza de Vaca. They pointed to the danger of losing contact with the ships, their only means of returning to lands known to be occupied by their countrymen. And from the vantage point of a survivor's hindsight in 1542, Cabeza de Vaca would insist that he had adamantly opposed Narváez's decision to divide the expedition when a proven port and rendezvous point to the north had not been established. But dissent was to no avail. Don Pánfilo was governor of the land and commander of the company. The men and women on ships and land would do as he ordered.[41]

Nevertheless, because Cabeza de Vaca had joined a minority of those who questioned the commander's good judgment, Narváez apparently sought to humiliate don Álvar by suggesting that he could stay with the

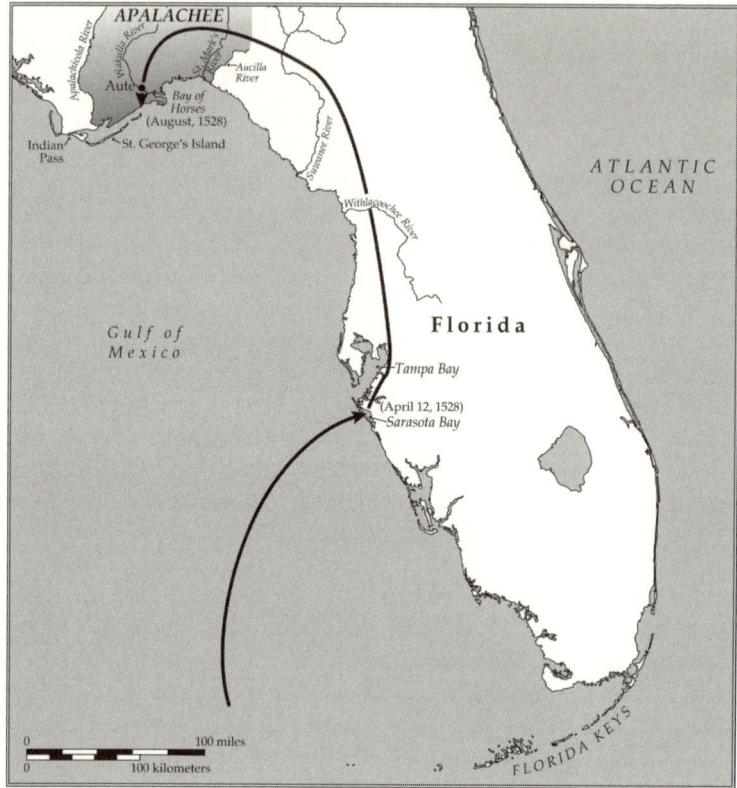

Figure 3. Route by sea and land of the Pánfilo de Narváez Expedition, 1528. Cartography by Mapping Specialists, Fitchburg, Wisconsin. Courtesy Andrés Reséndez.

ships and take command there if he were so reluctant to join the inland party. This was an affront to Cabeza de Vaca's pride, with clear implications of cowardice. He angrily stated that to suggest his remonstrances had been motivated by fear placed his character "under attack, and that I preferred risking my life to placing my honor in jeopardy."[42]

Among members of the expedition who expressed opposition to the governor's plan were some ten wives aboard the ships whose husbands had been picked for the overland exploration. They understandably faced an uncertain future if their husbands never returned. One outspoken woman even urged her female companions to consider themselves abandoned, because their husbands would surely perish, and she further urged them to seek the immediate protection of crew members.[43]

The inland party, as some had feared, would never again make contact with the support vessels. All attempts by those on horseback and afoot to find a suitable port where the ships might be anchored failed. As for the ships themselves, they often had to remain well offshore to avoid running aground on the Florida coast. Nevertheless, the seaborne contingent continued a determined search for the trekkers that went on for nearly a year, including a return to Tampa Bay. At that juncture the vessels, with some of the women then proclaiming themselves widows, set sail for Cuba, leaving the inland expeditionaries to their fate—ultimately, a cruel one that awaited them.[44]

The march toward Apalachee began on May 1, with the trekkers' only rations being two pounds of biscuits and a half pound of salt pork per man—as it turned out, their sole sustenance for two weeks. Weakened by hunger and exhausted by having to cross streams by swimming, canoeing, and rafting, the men finally came upon about two hundred Indians. The Spaniards seized half a dozen natives and followed them to their houses, about a mile and a half away. There they found large quantities of corn ready for harvesting, which they feasted on while giving thanks to God rather than to their human providers.[45]

Later, entreaties urging Narváez to march to the coast and remain there for a possible rendezvous with the support vessels were ignored. His sights were set on reaching Apalachee and its promise of riches. Several days beyond the appropriated corn harvest, an Indian lord, borne on the shoulders of stout porters, and his retinue of followers boldly approached the marchers. The chieftain and Narváez, much handicapped by communication only in signs, parlayed for an hour. What transpired suggested to the Spaniard that these Indians were bitter enemies of those at Apalachee and more than willing to lead him to that locale. So the trekkers followed their guides for a month and a half. During this time, the first of what would be an appalling number of Spanish fatalities occurred when a cavalryman and his horse drowned while crossing a large river. For the marchers, the loss of a companion was softened by their feast on horse meat.[46]

In mid-June 1528, the foot-sore and fatigued company caught sight of Apalachee. With clear evidence of many foodstuffs available and the expectation of finding much gold, the men cheered their good fortune. Even the spirits of Cabeza de Vaca, who had continued to grouse about losing contact with the ships, were buoyed: "On finding ourselves where we desired to be . . . it seemed to us that a great portion of our hardship and weariness had been lifted from us."[47] It was to be a short-lived sentiment.

Apalachee was apparently the most populous and richest region in

Florida, but its bounty in corn, seafood, and game animals was far from what Narváez and his men had hoped to find. And they would soon discover that Apalachee was no Aztec empire with gold and precious gems for the taking. Worse, from the Spaniards' viewpoint, the area was so populous that it had an all-powerful chieftain "associated with the life-giving sun." His leadership and the sheer number of Indians armed with bows and arrows made their situation more precarious. Finally, there was no city called Apalachee, instead it was only the name of a region. There was, however, a capital village called Anhaica, which Narváez and his men would never see, because the chieftain whom they soon took hostage led them toward one of the poorer regions of the province.[48]

The expeditionaries arrived at a place called Aute, near the mouth of the Wakulla River in the Florida panhandle, having suffered attacks by Indian archers along the way that killed both men and horses. The nearby coast had coves and swamps with offshore barrier islands, as well as massive oyster reefs that extended far out to sea. Waist-deep water made it unlikely that ocean-going vessels could be seen or hailed from their camp. After months of exhaustive marching and at times fatal brushes with Indians, "the survivors had reached a cruel dead end." Cabeza de Vaca spoke of their despair and gloom with these words: "I refrain here from telling this at greater length, because each one can imagine for himself what could happen in a land so strange and so poor and so lacking in every single thing that it seemed impossible to be in it or to escape from it." It had been exactly four months since the trekkers had left the ships near Tampa Bay.[49]

Narváez and his followers spent another month and a half at their camp, deciding what to do and how to go about it. They named their encampment the Bay of Horses, because every third day they killed a horse and cooked its meat over open fire. To their credit, they worked constantly under severe hardships at building crude rafts, deemed the best means of egress from the estuary and for travel along the Gulf Coast toward the Río de las Palmas.

Many are the accounts of Anglo Americans in United States history who took pride in their resourcefulness, at times called Yankee ingenuity. However, Spaniards forced to "make do" under dire circumstances were equally innovative. Among the survivors, then numbering slightly fewer than 250 of the original 300, was only one carpenter. Nonetheless, the men coped well. They jury-rigged bellows of deerskin and wooden pipes to melt iron from their crossbows, bridle bits, and stirrups; they cast molten metal into crude axes and saws for felling and sectioning trees; they turned flayed and tanned horsehide into fresh water bags; they used

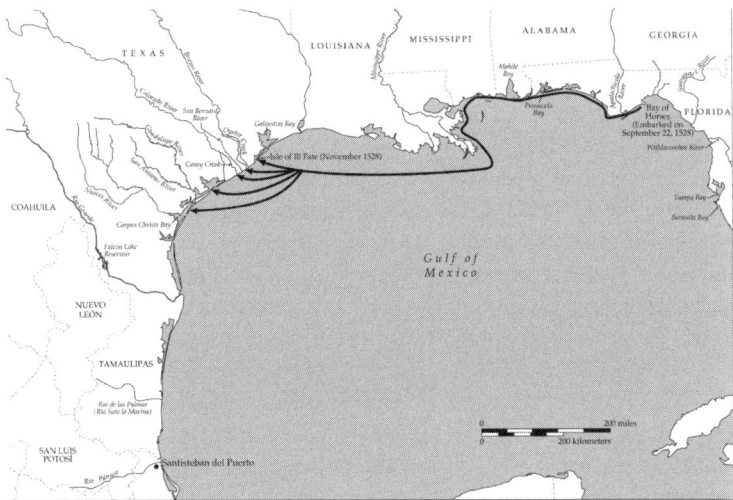

Figure 4. Route of five rafts launched by the Pánfilo de Narváez Expedition, 1528. Cartography by Mapping Specialists, Fitchburg, Wisconsin. Courtesy Andrés Reséndez.

strips of leather, braided horse hair, and pine resins to bind logs together and caulk the gaps; they wove hair from horses' manes and tails into rigging; and they fashioned their shirts and trousers into sails.[50] All was in preparation for leaving northwest Florida by sea (see Figure 4).

Eleven years later, members of the Hernando de Soto expedition would arrive at the Bay of Horses and remark on the great piles of bones and skulls of horses. They likewise commented on nearby groves of pine trees interspersed with hacked and scarred stumps. It must have been a sobering sight for Spaniards who would later wander through the land of several southeastern states of the United States before setting foot on Texas soil in 1542.

When Narváez and his companions had finished building the five rafts, each was perhaps a bit more than thirty feet in length, and each would contain just fewer than fifty men. The loaded platforms rose about seven inches above water line, with provisions consisting of food, clothing, and fresh water stored in tanned leather stripped whole from the legs of horses. Their departure date was September 22, 1528.[51]

It took several days for the rafts to clear inlets and shallows before reaching open waters of the Gulf, which the men feared because it placed them "in a sea so treacherous and without any one ... having any knowledge of the art of navigation." On reaching an offshore island, the Spaniards were able to appropriate mullet and dried fish eggs from Indians who fled their approach, leaving behind food items desperately needed by the Europeans and Africans. Another pressing need would soon be fresh water, because that stored in "vessels that we had made from the legs of horses later rotted," whereupon they either leaked their precious contents or rendered them undrinkable.[52]

On reaching a second small island, the men searched in vain for fresh water but were forced to remain there for six days because they feared a great storm that had overtaken them. For five of those days they had no fresh water. Their thirst was such that some of the men, driven half mad, began gulping sea water. In the words of Cabeza de Vaca, "five men died on us." Despite worries that the unabated storm would swamp their rafts, the men took to sea again in a desperate search for drinkable water. As luck would have it, they reached a shoreline inhabited by seemingly friendly Indians who shared cooked fish and fresh water stored in containers.[53]

All seemed well with these Indians, but in the middle of night they suddenly attacked the Spaniards. One of the assailants hurled a rock at Narváez that struck him in the face, but at least he kept his one good eye. The Indians also attacked the sick who lay scattered along the shore, and from evidence recorded later, it appears that five Spaniards died from three coordinated assaults. Cabeza de Vaca also numbered among the casualties, having suffered a wound to his face. As the exhausted men retreated into an estuary, a canoe filled with Indians approached the governor's raft and offered to bring him fresh water if he would give them something to carry it in, which he did. When the Indians left, two Christians accompanied them of their own volition. However, according to Cabeza de Vaca, when the natives returned to the rafts at night, they "brought our vessels without water."[54] It was a brazen act of defiance and ill will for the strangers, and the Indians refused to return the two Christians, whom they held captive.

On the following morning, the Spaniards found their rafts surrounded by Indians in many canoes. The Indians tried to lure them ashore by promising water and food but still refused to return the two Christians. Worse, the canoes seemed to be heading to a point that would have blocked the mouth of the estuary, leaving the Spaniards at a disadvantage with the Indians. The expeditionaries turned sailors quickly saw the danger and began paddling toward the open sea, assailed by Indians hurling stones from slings and spears launched by hand. It seems, however, that what the Indians wanted was for the Spaniards to leave, because they did not use their few but more lethal bows and arrows. And so the raft-borne men escaped, continued west, and soon arrived at the mouth of the Mississippi River.[55]

The river's current was strong, and where it entered the sea as a freshet the men soon drank their fill. This, however, marked a turning point for them. Soon after passing the Mississippi's debouchment, a strong norther blew the rafts seaward to where land could not be seen at times—a most disturbing happenstance for Spaniards in unseaworthy vessels. And for the first time, everyone suffered from cold. In desperation, the weakened men took to their oars. After two days of battling winds and currents difficult to read, the Spaniards "saw many spires of smoke along the coast." But as night had approached, they dared not risk landing in the dark.[56]

What seemed prudent, in fact, resulted in the five rafts becoming separated in the night due to strong offshore winds. And at no point in the future would all five vessels be in view of each other. The raft bearing Cabeza de Vaca did manage to approach two others, one of which was that of the governor. Cabeza de Vaca urged Narváez that they make an all-out effort to find the two missing craft, but the governor dismissed his suggestion. Don Álvar was advised that "I should have my men take their oars and row, because only by the strength of arms could land be taken."[57]

Narváez's advice to Cabeza de Vaca echoed what he himself planned to do, "but since the governor carried the healthiest and robust men among us," in the opinion of Cabeza de Vaca, "in no way were we able to follow or keep up with him." Don Álvar then asked if he could attach a line to the governor's raft so that the two craft could make landfall by night. His request was denied, because Narváez saw that a raft with its weakened crew tied to his would greatly lessen his chances of reaching land and safety. In desperation, Cabeza de Vaca, believing his own chances of making landfall slim, asked the governor what he thought he should do. Narváez's reply speaks volumes about the man as a commander— "he answered me that it was no longer time for one man to rule another, that each one should do whatever seemed best to him in order to save his own life, [and] that he intended so [sic] to do it."[58] Soon after, the governor's raft veered away and was lost from view, leaving Cabeza de Vaca and his men on their own.

It is probably fair to view Pánfilo de Narváez as an irresolute commander who denied aid to his followers to save his own skin. In earlier years during the conquest of Mexico, he had likewise proved to be a less than competent captain. He was incautious, if not headstrong, in dividing his expedition into maritime and land components in an uncharted land. Although severely handicapped by faulty geographic information on the Gulf Coast and the location of the Río de las Palmas, Narváez's leadership nonetheless falls well short when compared to Spanish captains such as Hernando Cortés, Francisco Vázquez de Coronado, or Hernando de Soto.

Left to the fate that awaited Cabeza de Vaca and others on his raft, it is remarkable that they survived. The time of year at this juncture, by don Álvar's calculation, was winter, although in reality it was late autumn. Still, he remarked on "the cold very great" and the piteous condition of weakened and starving men in his raft having "fallen on top of one another . . . so close to death that few were conscious." Indeed, in the entire raft, "there were not five men left standing."[59]

Throughout the last night at sea, only Cabeza de Vaca and the helmsman were able to take turns at the tiller. Near dawn, don Álvar was heartened by the sound of surf pounding on a nearby shore. He waited until better light, and then rowed with all his might toward land. Near shore, "a wave took us that pitched the raft out of the water the distance of a horseshoe's throw, and with the great blow that its fall occasioned, almost all the people who were nearly dead upon it regained consciousness." The aroused men left the raft "half walking, half crawling" and arrived on Texas soil, although it was assuredly an island, not the mainland.[60]

CHAPTER 3

THE HISTORY OF TEXAS, as recorded by a European observer, begins with the recollections of Cabeza de Vaca on November 6, 1528. On this date, the raft bearing him and perhaps forty-five others "shipwrecked," to don Álvar's way of thinking, on an island off the Texas coast. Cabeza de Vaca entitled his *Relación* (*Account*) *Naufragios* (*Shipwrecks*), first published in 1542. In it, he described what transpired on the cold autumn morning that marked the end of his voyage by raft. That platform of logs, lashed together and launched a month and a half earlier on the coast of Florida, could hardly be classified as a "ship," but it had served Cabeza de Vaca well—especially given that his conveyance for just less than the next eight years would be his legs.

Other than the date on which Cabeza de Vaca arrived on the soil of the future Lone Star State, the site itself being an island, and that this same isle beached another of the five rafts, little else is agreed upon by those who have attempted to trace his experiences from on or near Galveston Island to Mexico City in 1536. On that epic journey, he would later be accompanied by two other Spaniards and an African-born slave who were aboard the second raft.

The literature dealing with the route followed by Cabeza de Vaca— above all the portion of it that was within Texas—is considerable in volume and, as implied, controversial in nature. This small book is not the place to delve into the thorny thicket of scholarly disputation, which is mild compared to the exaggerated claims of Texas "nationalists" and local boosters (those who think all things "Texas" are bigger and better than elsewhere or happened in their locale). Accordingly, not all route interpretations are equally valid, although none can claim absolute certainty. The reader is therefore advised that in this volume where route interpretation is important to Cabeza de Vaca's odyssey, it will be based in large measure on my article published in the *Southwestern Historical Quarterly*.[61]

Whether the landfall island was Galveston or Folletts to the west is important for identifying the Indians who soon arrived. If Galveston, they were more likely Hans (Atakapas); if Folletts, they were more likely Karankawas or Akokisas. It is here believed to have been Folletts. In short order, about one hundred Indian archers confronted the Spaniards. Karankawas were known to have been tall in stature when compared with other Texas Indians, but Cabeza de Vaca is not much help here in identifying the Indians. In his words, "whether or not they were of great stature, our fear made them seem like giants." He added, "it was out of the question for us to think that anyone could defend himself, since it was difficult to find even six who could raise themselves above the ground."[62]

Cabeza de Vaca named the landfall island Malhado, or Isle of Misfortune. The name is appropriate for the fate of many who arrived on the two rafts, not because of any ill treatment by the Indians, who could hardly have been more accommodating under the circumstances. In response to small gifts of glass beads and hawk bells, they gestured that they would return on the following day with food, because at that time they had none. The Indians were faithful to their promise, bringing fish and edible roots, as well as fresh water in containers over the course of the next few days.

Encouraged by supplies of food and water, the men dug the raft out of the sand and tried to relaunch it, but their efforts ended in disaster. Only a short distance from shore, a huge wave overturned the raft and trapped three men beneath it—all of whom drowned. Those who escaped were drenched with sea water and "naked as the day we were born and [we had] lost everything we carried with us." Cabeza de Vaca described the survivors as so gaunt that without difficulty they could count every bone in their bodies and all appeared as "the figure of death itself." Shivering from hypothermia, the men managed to light a fire and crowd around it for warmth.[63]

Near sunset the Indians, unaware that the Spaniards had tried to leave by water earlier in the day, returned to check on them and again brought food. Upon seeing Cabeza de Vaca and his companions, all naked and miserable: "The Indians . . . began to weep loudly and so sincerely that they could be heard a great distance away." And then don Álvar added words that truly summed up their plight: "To see that these men, so lacking in reason and so crude in the manner of brutes, grieved so much for us, increased in me and others of our company even more the magnitude of our suffering."[64] In short, if the Indians felt sorry for *them, they* with their notions of Christian and European superiority, the Spaniards knew they were in trouble!

But their despair was soon mitigated when Cabeza de Vaca and his companions encountered other members of the expedition on Malhado, whom they had not seen since losing sight of them near the mouth of the Mississippi River. In all, the Europeans and their African slaves probably numbered around eighty-four men. The raft on which the other party had arrived was still intact, but in attempting to launch it, the logs fell apart and drifted away. Believing that the Río de las Palmas must surely by then be close by, four robust men known to be good swimmers were sent down the coast in hope of rescue from New Spain. All would die on the Texas coast.

Those who remained on Malhado, as well as the Indians who assisted them, soon fell ill. It has long been assumed that members of the Narváez expedition spread deadly European pathogens to the Indians living near Galveston Island. On careful analysis, this appears not to have been the case. First, there is no evidence of Indians in Florida having been afflicted with Old World diseases borne by the Narváez company. And, because the Spaniards had spent some forty-five days at sea before arriving on the Texas coast, it is unlikely that anyone aboard the rafts would have had an infectious disease that had not run its course, thereby rendering it non-transmittable. Second, whatever the illness, more Spaniards than Indians died of it. Only 19 percent (fifteen) of the eighty Spaniards survived. Thus an 81 percent mortality rate among the Europeans suggests the possibility of "virgin soil epidemic in reverse," especially given that the North American continent prior to Columbus's arrival was far from a disease-free Eden.[65]

Remarkably, all five rafts made landfall on the Texas coast, and the men on the other three fared worse than those who survived disease on Malhado. One of the craft came ashore west of Folletts Island near the mouth of the San Bernardo River; another, farther west near the mouth of Caney Creek; and the last, approximately one hundred miles farther on Matagorda Island. The raft grounded near Caney Creek contained Narváez and somewhat fewer than four dozen others (see Figure 5). The governor, having earlier renounced his command, then attempted to reassert control over any survivors from the other craft. He also feared an Indian ambush and arrogated to himself the privilege of sleeping on the raft with only a helmsman and servant, while others had to bed down on shore. It was his undoing. Around midnight, a strong norther blew the raft, grappled with only a rock, from shore without the men awakening, "and nothing more was ever heard of it." As historian Andrés Reséndez has remarked, "Against all odds, Narváez would not die of an Indian attack or a debilitating illness. Instead, in a supreme final irony, he spent his final hours con-

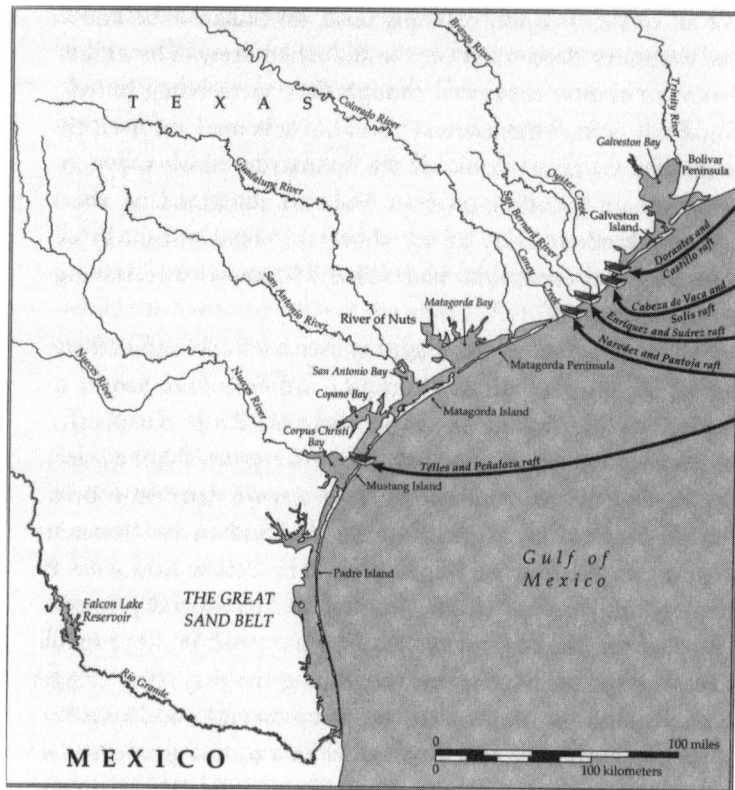

Figure 5. Landing sites of five rafts and their principal occupants on the Texas coast, 1528. Cartography by Mapping Specialist, Fitchburg, Wisconsin. Courtesy Andrés Reséndez.

fined on a small platform floating on the Gulf of Mexico and surrounded by the enormous . . . [land] that he had failed to conquer."[66]

Again, all of the Spaniards traveling on the third, fourth, and fifth rafts lost their lives on the Texas coast—some starved to death, others died of disease, and still others fell to Indian arrows or clubs. As Cabeza de Vaca reported, some Texas Indians killed the Spaniards "for their own amusement,"[67] others killed the strangers because they were competitors for food, and still others killed because the Europeans were "other," while they were "self." Indian groups in North America almost invariably referred to themselves in their language as "The People." Those not of "The People" were "other," often labeled as barbarians or sub-humans. None of this should surprise the reader. Indians were just like all human beings, which is to say potentially dangerous but also capable of remarkable compassion, as they demonstrated for Spaniards on Malhado. And Spaniards themselves assuredly regarded Indians as "other."

In the winter of 1528–29, Cabeza de Vaca, thanks to gifts of food and water given by the Indians, had recovered his health and strength to where he could travel to the mainland. There, however, he fell ill and remained near death for some time. By spring the fourteen survivors on Malhado somehow received word that Cabeza de Vaca had died. Then, encouraged by warmer weather, all but two of them proceeded down the coast toward the Río de las Palmas. Among those who departed were Alonso del Castillo, Andrés Dorantes, and the African slave Estevanico, all future companions of Cabeza de Vaca, but not before some four years would pass.

Since Cabeza de Vaca had much time to himself, he came to know the shoreline people and island dwellers better, and he remembered interesting things about them. They not only decorated their bodies with red ochre, but the men also pierced their lower lip and inserted a thin reed in it. Their women, as he put it, "are given to hard work." But both men and women, he added, "love their children more and treat them better than any other people in the world. And when it happens that one of their children dies, the parents and the relatives and all the rest of the people weep. And the weeping lasts a whole year."[68]

Cabeza de Vaca and a few others unwillingly gained some stature with the Indians as doctors. In his words, "they tried to make us physicians without examining us or asking for our titles." Since the Indians believed their afflictions could be cured by blowing on them and by touching with hands, they insisted that he and other Spaniards do likewise. When they refused, laughing and mocking such ministrations as quackery, the Indians "took away our food until we did as they told us."[69]

In treating the ill, Cabeza de Vaca added a Catholic touch by making the sign of the cross over a malady, by blowing on it, and then by reciting a Pater Noster and Ave Maria. He followed this with a fervent prayer that God in his mercy would grant health to the infirm and in doing so move the Indians to treat him well. If the ministrations worked or seemed to work, the natives were so grateful that they gave up eating for a time so as to provide him with victuals, as well as skins and other items.[70]

Although Cabeza de Vaca's treatment of sick Indians gave him some stature, he soon fell on hard times. He noted that his sickness on the mainland prevented him from returning to Malhado for more than a year, and during that time he was enslaved by unidentified natives and forced to do exhausting tasks. Among them was the Indians' insistence that he dig roots submerged in water and amid rushes. The reeds had sharp edges that cut his fingers and caused bleeding. Since he performed these labors "naked as the day he was born," his entire body was exposed to scratches and lesions.

Cabeza de Vaca eventually escaped from these Indians and the hard life he endured as their slave. He then became a merchant and found this occupation much to his liking. Don Álvar carried items found on the coast, such as conch shells and "beads of the sea" (probably pearls), into the interior. There inland groups especially valued the shells, which they used to cut open mesquite beans. From inland Indians he acquired animal skins and red ochre, the latter much valued by coastal people for body decorations. Cabeza de Vaca liked being a merchant because the Indians gave him food for his wares, he was not enslaved, he went where he chose, and most importantly he could learn about the land and be "able to seek out the way by which I would go forward."[71]

For approximately three years, Cabeza de Vaca continued his travels as the first European merchant in Texas. It is not possible from his *Account* to identify the inland areas that he visited or gauge how far he might have traveled, but this has not stopped modern-day boosters and Texas nationalists from insisting that he trod the soil of this or that Texas county. In these travels and later ones, about half of Texas's 254 counties have claimed his long-ago presence. The late Dan Kilgore, Corpus Christi native and former president of the Texas State Historical Association, some years ago told me that he had arrived at this number of Texas counties claiming a visit by Cabeza de Vaca, and that he had even talked to one booster who insisted that don Álvar had walked down the future left side of main street in Big Spring, Texas! One thing, however, *is* well accepted about Cabeza de Vaca during this time. For three successive winters he returned to Malhado, because he did not ply his trade in that season, and he refused to abandon the two Spaniards who had chosen to remain on the island.

Each spring he pleaded with his fellow Spaniards to "go in search of Christians"—meaning to follow the coast as the dozen survivors had earlier chosen to do. Finally, near the end of the fourth year, one of the Spaniards on Malhado died. The dead man's companion was Lope de Oviedo, and Cabeza de Vaca finally convinced him it was necessary to leave the island—not an easy matter since Oviedo did not know how to swim and greatly feared drowning. But Cabeza de Vaca agreed to take the reluctant Spaniard on his back when they had to cross a number of inlets and four streams.

Cabeza de Vaca's mention of the four streams gives important credence to his narrative, and clearly places him on the upper Texas coast. The waterways were Oyster Creek, the Brazos River, the San Bernardo River, and Caney Creek. Don Álvar mentioned that the second named stream flowed directly into the Gulf without entering a bay, and "at no other place between the Río Grande and the Mississippi" is there another waterway that discharges directly into the Gulf.[72]

After crossing Caney Creek, Cabeza de Vaca and Lope de Oviedo arrived at a huge inlet about three miles wide and deep throughout. Across this expanse of water Indians could be seen who soon approached the two Spaniards. They informed Cabeza de Vaca and Oviedo "that farther ahead there were three men like us, and they told us their names." The men, of course, were Alonso del Castillo, Andrés Dorantes, and Estevanico. When the two Spaniards inquired about the other nine men who had left Malhado four years earlier, they were informed that all were dead.[73]

These Indians informed Cabeza de Vaca that the natives who held their surviving companions were "very idle and cruel," and that they kicked, slapped, and beat the three men. "And in order that we might see that what they had told us about the bad treatment of the others was true . . . they gave my companion slaps and blows, and I did not lack my share, and they threw mud balls at us, and each day placed arrows at our hearts, saying that they wanted to kill us as they had killed our other companions." This was too much for the faint-hearted Oviedo, who, despite Cabeza de Vaca's pleadings, turned back in the company of some Indian women and disappeared from history.[74]

Two days after Lope de Oviedo had departed, Cabeza de Vaca traveled on to the "River of Nuts," the present-day Guadalupe. The nuts, as described by don Álvar, were pecans. He thought them similar in size to walnuts in Spain, and his comment that the trees that produced them only bore fruit every other year provides further evidence.

An Indian informed Cabeza de Vaca that in a different area of the pecan grove he would find the other Christians. So he briefly stole away from his captors and ventured to the edge of the woods where he encountered Andrés Dorantes. The latter was astonished to see Cabeza de Vaca, having believed he had died four years earlier on the mainland. Both men "gave many thanks to God upon finding ourselves reunited, and this day was one of the days of greatest pleasures that we had had in our lives." Their joy was soon shared by Alonso del Castillo and Estevanico who arrived a bit later.[75]

Dorantes and Castillo then asked Cabeza de Vaca what his intentions were, and he replied that it "was to go to the land of Christians and that on this path and pursuit I was embarked." Dorantes told Cabeza de Vaca that he had long beseeched Castillo and Estevanico to do just what don Álvar had voiced, but since neither of the men could swim, they greatly feared crossing rivers and inlets. However, with two swimmers in their party and their promise to help the two who were not, escape was now possible.

And so the three Spaniards and the African reached an accord. Their agreement to flee their captors had to be kept in absolute secrecy, or the Indians would surely kill them if their intentions became known. Dorantes, Castillo, and Estevanico informed Cabeza de Vaca that he and they would have to wait six months before attempting escape. At that time, from about April to September of 1533, the Indians would move much farther south to feast on the fruit (tunas) of prickly pear cactus. This would place the four men temptingly close, or so they believed, to Christian lands to the south, which was the goal of all those who had sailed from the coast of Florida some four years previous.[76]

CHAPTER 4

CABEZA DE VACA, Alonso del Castillo, Andrés Dorantes, and Estevanico, often referred to as the Four Ragged Castaways, would spend approximately thirty more months in the future Lone Star State (early autumn 1532 to the first months of 1535) before crossing the Río Grande into Mexico. During twenty of those months, the men would be enslaved by Texas Indians. It is this two and a half years in the life of Cabeza de Vaca that establishes him as Texas's earliest historian, its first ethnographer, and its initial observer of native flora and fauna—all added to his "first" as a European merchant.

Of all Cabeza de Vaca's signal accomplishments as the earliest European observer of things "Texas," none comes close in importance to his first-hand descriptions of its Indians. At the Guadalupe River, three of the four men had been claimed by two Indian groups. The Yguaces (Coahuiltecans) held Castillo and Estevanico; the Mariames (also Coahuiltecans) claimed Dorantes. Without question, a large portion of very early ethnographic information on Coahuiltecan people comes from Cabeza de Vaca's *Account*. Indeed, the long-time "giants" of Texas anthropologists, W. W. Newcomb Jr. and the late Thomas N. Campbell, both praised him. Newcomb credited him with knowing more about the hunting and gathering coastal Indians "than any other European or American ever did afterward." Similarly, Campbell, likewise with a bit of hyperbole, noted that Cabeza de Vaca "looms large as an ethnographer" and that the cultural information in his *Relación* is superior to that in all other sources combined.[77]

Cabeza de Vaca named seventeen Indian groups living in the area from the lower Guadalupe River southwestward to the Río Grande. Four were shoreline residents between the Guadalupe and San Antonio Bay; eleven were south of San Antonio Bay, occupying a region along a northeast-southwest shoreline axis; and two apparently lived west of the sand plain of present-day Brooks and Kenedy counties.[78] As anthropologist Campbell noted, Cabeza de Vaca lived among these Indians and later described them in published format. No other Spaniard was able to do that. His ethnographic information on the Coahuiltecans is especially important, because after leaving Texas in early 1535, it would be nearly two hundred years before Spaniards would learn significantly more about Coahuiltecans at the mission sites of San Juan Bautista and San Antonio. By that time, many of the Indian groups described by Cabeza de Vaca no longer existed.

Cabeza de Vaca obviously had little choice in the early 1530s about where he would live or the opportunities accorded him to observe Coahuiltecan cultures. He would have to go where his captors took him, as would the other three men. But the two Spaniards and lone African had lived long enough among the Mariames and Yguaces to learn about their seasonal movements. And this figured importantly in planning their escape strategy.

During early to late summer, both groups moved south toward the lower Nueces River and beyond to feast on tunas. Prickly pear cactus in this region, which included parts of Live Oak, Duval, Jim Wells, Nueces, and Kleberg counties, then grew in great profusion. It attained the height of ten feet and bore its fruit in such abundance that the Indians could feast on it for four to five months, and at times even longer.[79]

When the tuna harvest played out, the Coahuiltecans moved to their northern winter range. At this juncture, the Castaways planned to flee south, while their captors would move in the opposite direction toward the Guadalupe River. There the Indians would feast on pecans in years when the trees bore nuts. If it was a barren year for nut production, they dug roots or lived on other fare described in vivid detail by Cabeza de Vaca.

The Mariames, who had enslaved Andrés Dorantes, also claimed Cabeza de Vaca, and he would spend his first six months with these Coahuiltecans in the interior regions of Texas. The sparseness of the Indians' homeland forced them to scramble and consume almost anything edible. Cabeza de Vaca noted that his captors ate virtually all things alive—ants, worms, salamanders, spiders, lizards, and venomous snakes—as well as some things that were not, such as rotten wood and deer dung. Additionally, they ate other items so repugnant to don Álvar that he refrained from mentioning them by name. One can only speculate on what those food items might have been! He also added that the Mariames were occasionally so hungry that if the land had stones they would eat them, too.[80]

At times the Indians ate more appealing fare, certainly in the view of Cabeza de Vaca. These items included mesquite beans, seeds, nuts, and berries. His captors also ate venison, and don Álvar marveled that their astonishing stamina allowed them to run down deer on foot by following the animals until they were exhausted and easy to kill. Like other hunting and gathering groups, the Mariames did not eat balanced meals on a day-by-day basis, but they had balanced diets because they received nutrients on a seasonal basis.[81]

To those of us who have never faced prolonged hunger, it is perhaps easy to be repulsed by the food items consumed by Coahuiltecan tribes, especially their resorting to "secondary harvest"—meaning, they picked out and ate foods like mesquite beans that passed whole through an animal's alimentary canal. But as anthropologists remind us, all present populations are the descendants of hunting and gathering people. However, this mode of life was in the far distant past of most Europeans and Africans—meaning that Cabeza de Vaca and his companions probably viewed Indians as not much different from domesticated animals. Such an attitude would have made it easy for them to disparage Coahuiltecans "and by implication to deny . . . [them] their essential humanity." Similarly, contemporary scholars striving for a more balanced assessment of hunting and gathering cultures like the Coahuiltecans have faced the enormous task of "loosening the cold, dead grasp that ignorance and misinterpretation have frozen on the image of these [people]."[82]

The Castaways as slaves probably ate less than their Indian masters. They also were hungrier because they refused to eat some of the same foodstuffs, so it must have excited them to see an animal as large as a bison. Cabeza de Vaca was the first European to describe these animals, which he called "cows" (see Figure 6). A single bison, the largest mammal in North America, would have provided enough meat to last an entire band for days. But Coahuiltecans had to hunt on foot with primitive bows and arrows and found it difficult to kill these animals. Nonetheless, on a few occasions Cabeza de Vaca reported that he had eaten bison meat, which he regarded as better than beef in Spain.[83]

Rarely, however, did Coahuiltecans in southern Texas have ample food of any kind, and Cabeza de Vaca reported their not having any for as long as four days. He nonetheless reported them to be "a very happy people; [and] in spite of the great hunger they have, they do not on that account fail to dance or make their celebrations and *areitos*."[84] The latter, ceremonial dances performed by Indians in the Caribbean Islands, Mexico, and Texas, varied but often included songs recalling great deeds of their ancestors and gods.

The happiness of the Coahuiltecans was greatly tempered by onslaughts of mosquitoes, hardly surprising to anyone who has camped in southern Texas. Cabeza de Vaca, with something of a naturalist's eye, iden-

Figure 6. Depiction of a North American bison as described by the Castaways. After Francisco Hernández, *Nova plantarvm, animalivm et mineralivm Mexicanorvm* . . . (Rome, 1651). Courtesy University of Texas Libraries, Benson Latin American Collection.

tified three genera of this noxious insect. In his words, all were "very bad and vexatious." "And in order to defend ourselves from them, we made around the edge of the group great bonfires of rotted and wet wood that would not burn but rather make smoke." Again, as modern-day campers can affirm, the downside to this form of mosquito repellent is just as described by Cabeza de Vaca: "All night long we did nothing but weep from the smoke that got in our eyes." Worse, from the view of don Álvar, it was he and the other enslaved Spaniard who had to keep the dampened wood burning and smoking throughout the night. But if he or Dorantes dozed off and an Indian pestered by mosquitoes awoke, "they would remind us with blows to return to light the fires." Like all humans, some Indians were more allergic to mosquito bites than others, and Cabeza de Vaca compared those unfortunates to the biblical Lazarus, afflicted with leprosy.[85]

As slaves of the Mariames, Cabeza de Vaca and Dorantes endured bad treatment and the food accorded them for six months but looked forward to the Indians' southward migration to the prickly pear range in spring 1533. There they hoped to rendezvous with Castillo and Estevanico and "put into effect the plan we had made" for escape, the first part of which came to pass and the second seemed hopeful. However, just when the Castaways were at the point of fleeing, their plans were dashed. The Yguaces and Mariames began fighting over a woman. They set upon each other with blows and sticks and in the melee "wounded one another in the head." Both tribes became so enraged that they marched off in different directions, taking their slaves with them, "and by no means were we able to reunite until the following year."[85]

It was during this next year that Cabeza de Vaca, who had survived so much illness and adversity, nearly lost his life due to ill treatment and great hunger. On three occasions he attempted escape from his harsh circumstances, and in each instance the Mariames tracked him down, beat him, and threatened to kill him. But he continued to learn more about his captors and added to his accomplishments as Texas's first ethnologist.

Cabeza de Vaca observed that the Mariames regularly killed their infant daughters and fed their bodies to dogs. When asked why they would do such an ostensibly cruel and irrational act, the Indians replied that it would violate incest taboos for females to marry within their tribe, because everyone was related by clan kinship. If, on the other hand, they allowed their daughters to grow up and marry outsiders, they would bear offspring for enemies who surrounded them and increase the strength of those adversaries.[87]

Cabeza de Vaca found his captors singularly lacking in character, given that they were often thieves, occasional drunkards, and always liars. He also documented sodomy and male homosexuality among the Mariames. The latter behavior moved him to remark that alternate lifestyle men "perform every activity pertaining to women" and "openly have another man for a wife."[88]

Remarkably, the year between the summers of 1533 and 1534 passed without fatal consequences for the African and the three Spaniards, and once again the Four Ragged Castaways found themselves together as their captors traveled south to the great stands of prickly pear cactus. Given their escape plan, they had to wait to the very end of the great *tunal*, just prior to the Indians moving north for some one hundred miles to their lower Guadalupe River range. In conversations with the other men, Cabeza de Vaca made it clear that if there were any reluctance on their part to try escape, he would go forward by himself toward the Río de las Palmas and Pánuco. There were no dissenters, and by don Álvar's reckoning they agreed to flee separately around September 1 when the moon became full.[89]

Dorantes, who had been a slave of the Mariames for about six years, was the first to slip away and become a fugitive. He was very fortunate to have run upon the Anagados, another Coahuiltecan group foraging in a more southerly part of the great tunal, who accepted him and treated him well. Castillo and Estevanico were the next to escape the Yguaces and join Dorantes, but Cabeza de Vaca was still absent. Despite considerable odds, all had found each other by around the middle of September. The Castaways had been extremely lucky, for at any time the Anagados could have returned them to their former masters.[90]

Although the prickly pear tunas were almost gone, the four men found just enough fruit to sustain them as they hurried southward toward the Río Grande. En route they spotted smoke in the distance and sent Estevanico ahead as scout. The African learned from a lone Indian that the smoke came from houses farther on, and the native agreed to carry a message to the dwellings' occupants that the Castaways were coming their way. Upon their arrival, the four men were accepted with friendly gestures and allowed to spend the night in houses.[91]

These Indians were Avavares who spoke a language different from the Mariames and Yguaces but still understood that tongue when used by the Castaways. Accordingly, the four men were able to communicate readily with their hosts. To the Castaways' surprise, the Avavares had heard of their ability to heal the sick and felt privileged to have them as guests, and this was the start of much good fortune for the men. The Indians offered them food and would continue to treat them well for the next several months.[92]

The Castaways could hardly believe their good luck, having suffered so much ill treatment and constant hunger as slaves; but they, as before, attributed their deliverance to divine intervention, not to their worldly hosts. Although they could not know it, the four men had reached a turning point in their North American odyssey. Never again would they be enslaved, and never again would they be among Indians and not feel safe. This was also an important juncture for them in that they started to see Indians in a different light, something they had not experienced since the kindness given them by natives on Malhado some six years earlier.

The key to the Castaways' change of circumstance lay in their success as healers, and all would eventually act in this capacity. Alonso del Castillo was the first to offer ministrations to the Avavares. When quartered among them, several came to him—all complaining of "a malady of the head, begging him to cure them." Don Alonso made the sign of the cross over those in pain and commended them to God. All stated that their afflictions had abated, and all showed their gratitude by bringing him many tunas and a piece of venison, which none of the Castaways could identify.[93] This underscores an interesting point. As mentioned earlier, the Mariames and Yguaces occasionally killed deer, but they evidently had never permitted their slaves to taste venison.

News of Castillo's successful treatments spread like wildfire among the Avavares, and they soon called on Cabeza de Vaca to effect similar cures, which again seemed to have turned out well. In gratitude, the Indians showered the men with pieces of venison, "and there were so many of them that we did not know where to put the meat." The Indians, grateful that so many of them had shed their aches and pains, began celebrations and areitos that went on for three days.[94]

At the conclusion of these festivities, the Castaways began asking questions of their hosts about lands that lay ahead to the south. And the news was not favorable. The Avavares informed them that they would encounter much cold in those regions and very few hides for warmth. There also would be no food because the prickly pear season had almost completely played out. So, in the words of Cabeza de Vaca, "seeing that winter and cold weather were already upon us, we decided to spend it [sic] with these Indians."[95]

The four Castaways lived with the Avavares for eight months, but during that time they and the Indians had to forage constantly for food. On one occasion, while Cabeza de Vaca was searching for fruit, he became separated from his Indian companions in the night and was lost for five days. He was barefoot and had no clothing or hides for warmth and nearly died of hypothermia. But again he credited God with his survival, because he amazingly found a tree aflame—likely from a lightning strike—and was able to carry burning embers with him as he continued his search for his Castaway and Indian companions. By this time, he was well familiar with northers that sweep down from Canada, bringing cold winds and precipitation in their wake. So he was thankful that "God took pity upon me, that in all this time the north wind did not blow, because otherwise it would have been impossible for me to survive."[96]

Once reunited with his Castaway companions and Indian friends, Cabeza de Vaca would later record interesting ethnographic information about other Indian groups, as well as the Avavares of southern Texas. In foraging for food, he mentioned contact with five other tribes, and among those of special interest were the Atayos and Susolas. Despite being at war, both groups searched for food in the same area "and shot arrows at each other every day." Not surprisingly, Castillo and Cabeza de Vaca were then called upon to treat the wounded and other sick people.[97]

According to Cabeza de Vaca, Castillo was a very timid physician and hesitated to treat Indians when the outcome was in doubt. He also worried that since it was invariably God who cured the sick and wounded, his ministrations would be hampered by his unatoned sins. So, it was primarily Cabeza de Vaca who was sought out by the Indians to treat their critically wounded or ill. In one case, he was called on to doctor a man seemingly dead, because he had no pulse and his eyes had rolled up into his head. Further, the Indians had already torn down his dwelling, a clear sign that they believed the owner dead. Nonetheless, Cabeza de Vaca prayed over the man, made the sign of the cross, and blew his breath on him. That same night, Indians informed him that the man he treated had stood up, walked, talked, and eaten.[98]

The main residence of the Castaways was always with the friendly Avavares, not the warring tribes that called on them to treat their casualties. At this point in the men's odyssey, Dorantes and Estevanico had not attempted any cures. However, the reputation of Cabeza de Vaca and Castillo as healers was soon so widespread that the Indians referred to all of them as "children of the sun." And demands for their ministrations became so great, in the words of Cabeza de Vaca, that: "We all became physicians, although in boldness and daring to perform any cure I was the most notable among them."[99]

During the Castaways' eight-month sojourn with the Avavares, perhaps the most bizarre of all ethnographic information on Texas Indians came to light from these people. The Avavares insisted that about fifteen or sixteen years earlier an evil being (called *mala cosa* by Cabeza de Vaca) who was small in stature had terrorized them. This "bad thing" was so bearded that the Indians could not clearly see his face, but he was unquestionably evil incarnate. With a flint knife he made incisions in the stomachs of Indians and pulled out their entrails. This awful creature also possessed remarkable curative powers in that he could place his hands over an incision and close it. He could also pull arms from their sockets and replace them with no permanent damage to the victim. Mala cosa's powers were so great that he could even raise dwellings in the air and then crash them back to earth.[100]

The Castaways reacted to stories about this evil being by laughing "a great deal about these things they told us, making fun of them." When the Indians averred the truth of this horrible creature's powers by bringing forward those who still bore the scars of his cuts, the Castaways turned the matter to their advantage. They told the Avavares that if "they believed in God our Lord and were Christians like us, they would not be afraid of him, nor would he dare to come and do those things to them, and they could be assured that as long as we were in the land, he would not dare to appear in it."[101]

But all was not well with the four men. In the eight months spent with the Avavares, they suffered periodic hunger for six of them. When spring 1535 arrived and the prickly pear cactus again bore fruit, they would take their leave of these kind Indians and move south toward the Río Grande, the Río de las Palmas, and the province of Pánuco. This leg of journey would soon take them from Texas soil and onto that of Mexico, where trekking for two of them would finally end in July 1536.

CHAPTER 5

DURING THE MONTHS AHEAD for the Castaways, their specialty among Indians lay in possessing seemingly remarkable curative powers, which has sparked interesting conjecture. How could their ministrations, which began by praying over the ill or wounded, followed by making the sign of the cross and concluded by blowing on afflicted parts of a body result in such salutary benefits? Even for those who believe in miracles as the appropriate explanation for such phenomenal occurrences, what about care delivered by lay persons, rather than by members of the clergy?

As historian Andrés Reséndez has remarked, "the Europeans had become convinced that their preternatural interventions reflected God's divine plan for North America." Accordingly, the Castaways were merely agents of God's will. But the Indians' views of the men they called "children of the sun" were also contributing factors. Within their own cultures, Indians had always believed that some individuals such as their shamans possessed supernatural powers, and the Castaways were certainly out of the ordinary. They looked different, they came from the direction of the rising sun and beyond the ocean, and they spoke an unintelligible language.[102] Just as some people's health improves by taking a placebo, the Indians came to believe that the Castaways had unique powers to cure their illnesses and injuries, and so it seems they did.

Cabeza de Vaca would later write in his *Relación* that everyone treated by the Castaways always claimed to feel better or improve afterward, but he pointedly never claimed to have performed any "miracles." The Spanish Inquisition was especially powerful in the sixteenth century, and it "closely scrutinized all manuscripts for their religious content and issued licenses only to those texts deemed compatible with established dogma." Anyone, other than those approved by the church, who claimed to have performed a miracle could be hauled before the Inquisition's Holy Tribunal and sentenced to severe punishment or banishment from Spanish realms.[103]

As Cabeza de Vaca previously noted, Alonso del Castillo was an especially humble Christian. To a lesser degree, the other Spaniards and the African also insisted that they were nothing more than God's obedient servants. But as the Castaways' reputation as healers traveled with them and even beyond over the next several months, the Indians of extreme southern Texas and northern Mexico believed the ministrations themselves had curative powers.

There is evidence that Estevanico, the first African of record in Texas, had been baptized as a Roman Catholic. He bore the diminutive name of Stephen (Esteban in Spanish), the first Christian saint, who was stoned to death around AD 35. Furthermore, if he were a Muslim, Spanish law would have forbidden his passage to the Indies.[104] Born in Azamor, a city in northwest Morocco, Estevanico was a slave of Andrés Dorantes. But he was separated from his Spanish master and enslaved again by the Yguaces. During his captivity, it must have been silently satisfying to Estevanico that his elite Spanish master had been reduced to the same level as he, that of bondage. Once reunited with the three Spaniards in late 1534, Estevanico was on a more equal footing with them, in that he often served as scout and mediator with the Indians of South Texas and later those in Mexico. He also practiced cures once the demand for such services was more widely sought by sick and wounded Indians. His not being a Spanish-born Old Christian—as opposed to converts known as New Christians—apparently made no difference in the outcome of his ministrations, and his European companions welcomed Estevanico's helping hand in treating the afflicted.

At the conclusion of eight lunar months, the Castaways said farewell to the Avavares, their friendly hosts whose range was southwest of Corpus Christi Bay. The four men's departure probably came in late spring 1535, because Cabeza de Vaca noted that it was about two weeks before the prickly pear tunas would ripen. They, however, wanted to travel during the warm months.[105]

The Castaways followed an inland route from the coast and its shoreline Indians, whose hostility to outsiders was well known, because they had killed every Spaniard who had not died of starvation, illness, or injury on three of the rafts. But the harsh interior *monte* (scrub country) also had its perils. Food was so scarce that the four trekkers traded some nets and a deerskin for two dogs, which they ate. But they suffered daily from thorn pricks all over their bodies, since they had no clothing. At this juncture, Cabeza de Vaca commented on the men's skin condition. They burned and peeled so often that he compared themselves to serpents in that "we changed our skins twice a year." Their backs were also ulcerated from carrying heavy loads that "caused the ropes to cut into our flesh."[106]

Cabeza de Vaca stated that in passing through spiny shrubs he shed so much blood that it called to his mind the Passion of the Christ. But he piously acknowledged so much greater was the suffering of the Redeemer "from the thorns, than that which I had to endure at that time." Nonetheless, he complained more about hunger than blood loss. The former was so intense that his best sustenance came when Indians gave him a hide to scrape and soften. Its meat scraps provided enough food to sustain him for two or three days of travel.[107]

The Indians encountered by the Castaways between their departure from the Avavares and their arrival at the Río Grande were all warlike and constantly fought one another. Some lured their enemies into ingenious ambushes. At night, women and children set up camp, lit fires, and perhaps feigned sleep, while men armed with deadly weapons hid in nearly gullies or covered themselves with brush—always at the ready to pounce on unwary assailants. The Indians were so resourceful and violent that they reminded Cabeza de Vaca of his youthful, first-hand experiences while soldiering in the Spanish army. In his opinion, the Indians of southern Texas were as adept and cunning in protecting "themselves from their enemies as they would have if they had been raised in Italy and in continuous wars."[108]

Life for these nomadic Indians was so filled with peril that they slept with bows strung and arrows at the ready. And with food sources undependable or in short supply, children nursed for six to ten years, or until they could forage on their own. At the same time, lactating mothers were often unable to conceive, thereby limiting population numbers and ensuring parity of dietary needs and available resources.

After several more days of trekking, the Castaways left the warring tribes and arrived at a large river, the Río Grande, which they forded and entered Mexico. Their point of crossing was likely near the present-day Falcón Lake Reservoir, as supported by sparse archeological data and by identification of populous Indian groups specific to that locale, who are mentioned in the *Account*.[109]

Shortly after the Castaways entered Mexico and reached the mountains, they departed from their long-stated goal of continuing south but inland from the coast toward the Río de las Palmas and Pánuco. Instead, they veered sharply to the west toward the Pacific Ocean. No one can state with certainty why the wayfarers arrived at this decision, but it likely involved these considerations: friendly Indians reminded them, although hardly necessary, that the shoreline Indians were very bad, while those in the interior were better disposed and possessed more food. Second, geographic considerations were important, because the four men had no way of knowing the great distance they would have to walk across northern Mexico to reach the Gulf of California. And, finally, as Cabeza de Vaca admitted, by traveling inland they also had an opportunity to discover new lands and collect important information.[110]

The Castaways' travels across northern Mexico toward the confluence of the Río Conchos and Río Grande were rapid and generally without unusual occurrences, with one notable exception. En route, Cabeza de Vaca performed the first recorded surgery in the North American Borderlands. The procedure involved removing the point of an arrow that had struck an Indian below the shoulder and come to rest above his heart. This had caused much distress and illness for the victim, and so don Álvar decided to open the man's chest and remove the arrowhead. In his words, "I saw that the point . . . was very difficult to remove. I again cut deeper, and I inserted the knife point, and with great difficulty, at last I pulled it out. It was very long and, with a deer bone, plying my trade as a physician, I gave him two stitches." "And two days later, I removed the two stitches and he was healed."[111] (see Figure 7)

In medical terminology, this procedure was a sagittectomy. It has earned Cabeza de Vaca lasting fame as the "Patron Saint" and symbol of the Texas Surgical Society, even though the operation was almost certainly performed in Mexico. Pedantry aside, his remarkable excision has earned him mention in a brief article appearing in the prestigious *New England Journal of Medicine*.[112] (see Figure 8)

During the entire portion of the Castaways' odyssey in northeast, north, and northwest Mexico before turning south near the Pacific coast, Cabeza de Vaca failed to remember or record the name of a single Indian group that he encountered. This was in dramatic contrast to the years he had spent in Texas when he recalled around two dozen specific tribal identities, all of which have been of great value to modern-day anthropologists and route interpreters. Had he named even one Indian group in northern Mexico, in the words of Thomas N. and Tommy Jo Campbell, "a trans-Texas route probably would not have been suggested by anyone."[113]

There is, nonetheless, a compelling piece of evidence to substantiate the trans-Mexico route that came to light in a 1997 publication. Cabeza de Vaca, while crossing a portion of the Sierra Madre Oriental, mentioned a locale identifiable from the *Account* that supported a growth of piñon

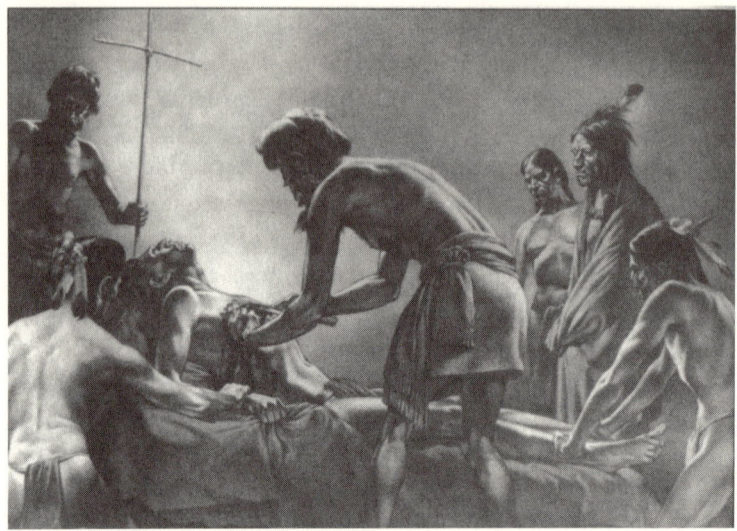

Figure 7. Depiction of Cabeza de Vaca's daring surgery in northern Mexico. Painting by Tom Lea. Courtesy of Moody Medical Library, University of Texas Medical Branch at Galveston.

Figure 8. Insignia of the Texas Surgical Society. Drawing by Tom Lea. Courtesy of the Texas Surgical Society, John W. Roberts, M. D., Secretary.

pines, which produced nuts with a shell so thin that he and his companions ate them whole. On-site identification of the rare *Pinus remota* was first confirmed on a field trip led by Donald W. Olson and Marilynn S. Olson at Southwest Texas State University in San Marcos (now Texas State University).[114]

In lands to the west beyond the paper-shell piñon harvest, news of the Castaways' success in curing illnesses and treating injuries swept before them, and they never traveled alone. Their crossing northern Tamaulipas and Coahuila, as Andrés Reséndez has remarked, may be described as "part processional, part doctor's visit, and part plunder." The men's Indian hosts were also very clever in suggesting that they deviate from their intended path toward one place or another with the hope of curing friends or relatives, while failing to help their enemies.[115]

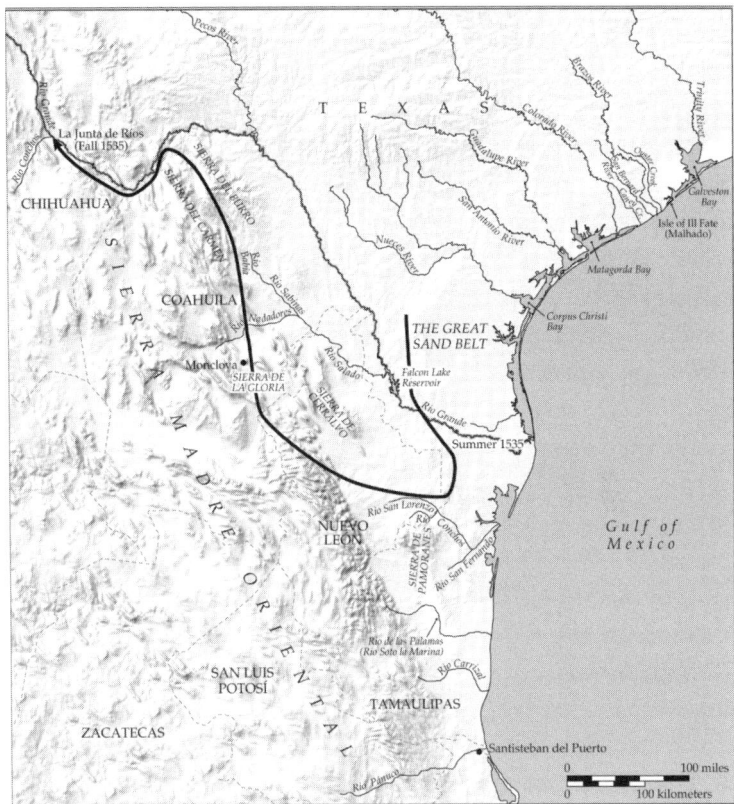

Figure 9. Path of the Castaways from their Río Grande crossing in South Texas to La Junta de los Ríos, 1535. Cartography by Mapping Specialists, Fitchburg, Wisconsin. Courtesy Andrés Reséndez.

Ironically, the four men who had fled slavery among the Mariames and Yguaces in Texas now moved at the head of throngs that may have numbered as many as three to four thousand. Their Indian followers kept the trekkers well fortified with food and water and accompanied them to the junction of the Río Grande and Río Conchos (La Junta de los Ríos) (see Figure 9). La Junta is located between the present-day towns of Presidio, Texas, and Ojinaga, Chihuahua; and the arrival there of the Castaways is agreed upon by virtually all route interpreters—with good reason. Almost fifty years later, a Spanish expedition would arrive at La Junta, and in conversations with elderly Indians learned that some of them remembered three Christians and a black man who had long ago passed among them.[116]

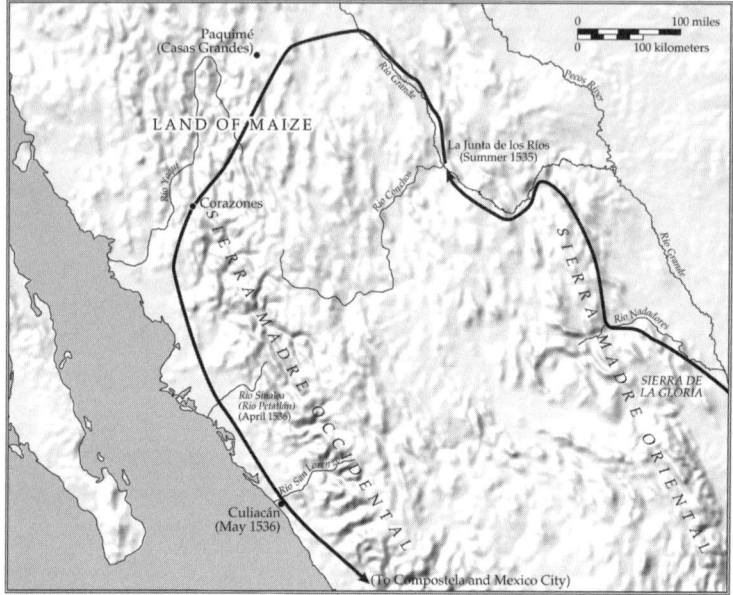

Figure 10. Path of the Castaways across northern Mexico to Corazones, Culiacán, Compostela, and continuation to Mexico City, 1535–1536. Cartography by Mapping Specialists, Fitchburg, Wisconsin. Courtesy Andrés Reséndez.

At the juncture of the two rivers, the wayfarers had reached an agricultural settlement where people lived in fixed houses and raised beans, squash, and maize, much to the joy of Cabeza de Vaca and his companions. Having found so much available food "was the thing that gladdened us more than anything else in the world, and for this we gave infinite thanks to our Lord."[117]

The Castaways spent several days among the Indians at La Junta, and then headed north by crossing the Río Grande. They ascended its left bank, or Texas side, for seventeen days and then re-crossed the river to the west, perhaps seventy-five miles downstream from modern-day El Paso, Texas. With this second crossing, they left Texas soil for the final time.[118]

Guided by friendly Indians, the Castaways continued westward for another seventeen to twenty days. They then veered sharply to the southwest and reached an area called the Land of Maize in northern Sonora (see Figure 10). Ahead lay the formidable Sierra Madre Occidental, and again with the assistance of Indian guides the men found a pass through the mountains. The travelers had traversed a region occupied by Indian cultures well advanced beyond any they had previously encountered.[119] On the western slopes of the Sierra Madre, the trekkers reached an area where the Indians also had permanent houses. The natives' material wealth included shoes, cotton blankets, and deerskin skirts. Of particular interest to the four men were items acquired by native merchants that included beads and corals from the Pacific Ocean, turquoises most likely from Pueblo country to the north, and "emeralds made into arrowheads from nearby deposits."[120] Rather than emeralds, these stones were probably malachite.

For the trekkers who had so often suffered from extreme hunger, at times going three to four days without food in southern Texas, the best was yet to come. At a village they appropriately called "*Corazones*"—"Hearts," the men received more than six hundred split and dried deer hearts. Even better, they would never again have to face prolonged hunger.

As the men continued toward the Pacific Ocean, known to them as the South Sea, their excitement would soon peak. Around Christmas 1535, and about seven months after leaving the friendly Avavares, Castillo's sharp eyes spotted a small belt buckle with a horseshoe nail attached to it. Worn as an amulet on a string around an Indian's neck, the buckle and iron nail were proof positive that they were Spanish in origin. Under questioning about the objects' origin, the Indians said they "had come from men who wore beards like us." The bearded ones had arrived on horses in the recent past and lanced two Indians.[121]

News of nearby Spaniards caused the men to hasten their pace, and they soon saw further evidence of their countrymen, such as tracks of horses and traces of camps. Cabeza de Vaca, Estevanico, and a few Indian comrades then forged well ahead of Castillo and Dorantes and soon came upon a small slave-raiding party north of San Miguel de Culiacán. According to Cabeza de Vaca, the four slavers, adherents of Governor Nuño de Guzmán in Nueva Galicia, were dumbstruck "upon seeing me so strangely dressed and in the company of Indians. They remained looking at me a long time, so astonished that they neither spoke to me nor managed to ask me anything."[122]

Cabeza de Vaca requested that the mounted Spaniards take him to where their captain resided. Upon meeting Diego de Alcazar, don Álvar informed him that Castillo and Dorantes in the company of many Indians were about thirty miles behind. With Estevanico as guide, three horsemen rode north to contact the larger party and escort them toward Culiacán. During that travel interim of about five days, Cabeza de Vaca asked for verification of the year, month, and date of his arrival. Although he did not record the precise date, it was probably early to mid spring 1536.[123]

When the full retinue of Indians rejoined the Castaways, the natives refused to believe that Cabeza de Vaca, Castillo, and Dorantes were of the same people as the dreaded slave raiders. The Indians' reaction underscores the important transformation that had occurred in their European and African friends, as well as the natives' *perception* of them. The strangers in many ways had melded themselves into the Indians' concept of "self," while the slave catchers were clearly "other." Cabeza de Vaca expressed their conviction with these words: "We [the Castaways] came from where the sun rose, and they [the slavers] from where it set; and that we cured the sick, and that they killed those who were well; and that we came naked and barefoot, and they went about dressed and on horses with lances; and that we did not covet anything but rather . . . that the others had no other objective but to steal everything they found and did not give anything to anyone."[124]

The key to how just a few mounted slave raiders could capture and control large numbers of Indians and force them into permanent enslavement lay in their horses. As Andrés Reséndez has observed, the arrival of Europeans in the Americas with their great advantage by traveling on horseback allowed them to dominate "an entire continent teeming with Indians who could not move faster than their own legs could carry them."[125] So, with the speed of their mounts, long lances for prodding, and whips for close-up punishment, half a dozen mounted men could burn villages, destroy crops, and literally "round up" dozens of men, women, and children and drive them some distance into servitude. With their crops ruined and homes destroyed, Indian men—reluctant to leave their wives and children—were disinclined to attempt escape.

As for the Castaways, now safe after some seven years of travail, life was about to change radically for one of them. Estevanico had been extremely important to the Spaniards' survival over months of time and many hundreds of miles of trekking. He was apparently as skilled as Castillo and Dorantes in treating Indian illnesses and injuries, and better than all the Spaniards as an advance agent and scout. Despite being a slave of Dorantes, Estevanico had morphed into a near-equal partner with the three Europeans during their North American odyssey. But once among Spaniards in settled portions of New Spain, he would quickly be reminded that he was still human chattel property—not fair, but that would be his condition.

Far better than the ill fortune that awaited Estevanico, Cabeza de Vaca would nevertheless not fare well among Spaniards for the remainder of his life. Brimming with confidence and the arrogance of a Spanish don, he had entered North America as treasurer and second in command of a major Spanish expedition. But after spending seven and a half years on the continent, during most of which he was either at the mercy of Indians near Malhado or as a slave of the Mariames, Cabeza de Vaca had emerged a changed man. He had learned a fundamental truth about Indians—not all were the same, just as his Indian friends in Nueva Galicia had discovered that not all Spaniards were alike.

CHAPTER 6

ONCE THE CASTAWAYS and the entourage of free Indians were re-united, the three Spaniards were safe among their countrymen. Their concern, however, lay with Indian friends, who perhaps numbered more than a thousand. All did their best to secure the natives' well-being, having helped deliver them into the hands of slave-hunting adherents of Governor Nuño de Guzmán. Unfortunately, the men could do nothing beyond pleas for the Indians' freedom, which were ignored by Captain Diego de Alcazar and his men.[126]

The wayfarers and natives were still some ninety miles from San Miguel de Culiacán. En route to the town, Alcazar's horsemen led the throng through a land devoid of Indian towns and ruined by slave raids. For two days they found no water and several Indians died of thirst before reaching Culiacán. Once there, the Castaways were well received by the captain of the province, Melchor Díaz, who apologized for their suffering and ill treatment by Captain Alcazar's mounted escort.[127]

The trekkers stayed at Culiacán for a few weeks, and then on May 15, 1536, were accompanied by twenty horsemen on a march of some three hundred miles to Compostela, the capital of Nueva Galicia. Much to the dismay of Cabeza de Vaca and his companions, they shared the passage with five hundred Indian slaves who were likely in chains.[128]

At Compostela the three Spaniards were graciously received by Nuño de Guzmán, who provided them with clothing from his own wardrobe. Cabeza de Vaca claimed that for several days he could not bear shirts and trousers touching his skin, and during that same time he was only comfortable sleeping on the ground. Once again the Castaways pleaded with Guzmán to free the Indians and allow them to live in peace. He ignored their entreaties and promptly dispatched them onward to Mexico City, where at last their trekking would end—some 2,400 miles from where they had fled from the Yguaces and Mariames in Texas.[129]

The four men arrived in the capital city on July 23, 1536, slightly more than seven and half years after touching Texas soil in November 1528. Among those who received them with great fanfare were Antonio de Mendoza, first viceroy of New Spain, and the famed conquistador, Hernando Cortés. Two days later on July 25, Cabeza de Vaca, Castillo, and Dorantes must have felt at home as they attended fiestas and bull fights and watched playful jousting on the Day of Saint James[130]—the most revered saint among Spaniards during the Spanish Reconquest and the conquest of the Americas.

To delighted audiences, the Castaways recounted their remarkable experiences in regions of North America unknown to other Europeans. What particularly piqued the interests of gold-hungry men in the capital were their accounts of lands far to the north that were rumored to have advanced civilizations and wealthy towns. In part, Cabeza de Vaca spurred this excitement by mentioning the "emerald" arrowheads given to him by people in the Land of Maize, which don Álvar carried for a time but lost in his travels. Second, the maize people's claims that the arrow points had come from rich lands beyond the mountains—assuredly reference to Pueblo country—rekindled hopes that the Seven Cities of Cíbola were within the reach of an enterprising sponsor.

Viceroy Antonio de Mendoza held the whip hand among those vying to organize and finance a follow-up expedition to the north. Despite the viceroy's best persuasive efforts, none of the Castaway Spaniards would agree to captain an *entrada* into lands from which they had escaped; however, Estevanico as a slave had no choice. He was either sold or his services were lent to the viceroy by Andrés Dorantes. The African would later serve as scout in early 1539 for an exploratory expedition to the north led by fray Marcos de Niza. Estevanico, again in his capacity as scout, soon ranged well ahead of the friar and arrived at a Zuni pueblo in western New Mexico. His demands there for turquoises and Indian women were a fatal mistake. Indian archers, as confirmed in a later report, shot him " full of arrows like a Saint Sebastián."[131]

Meanwhile, the three Spaniards in Mexico City drafted an account generally known as the Joint Report, or Oviedo Account, probably completed in late 1536.[132] The original manuscript is not extant, but it is believed to have been handed to Gonzalo Fernández de Oviedo, official historian of the Spanish Indies, in Cuba and included verbatim in his *Historia general y natural de las Indias*.[133] Logically, the recollections of three Castaways should be superior to one, that of Cabeza de Vaca, but this is not the case. With few exceptions, the Joint Report—assuming Oviedo copied it in its entirety—adds little new information to the published *Relación*, and it is a much briefer narrative.[134]

The three former Florida expeditionaries, Cabeza de Vaca, Castillo, and Dorantes, would soon part company. Viceroy Mendoza accepted Alonso del Castillo and Andrés Dorantes into his household and arranged their marriages to wealthy widows whose husbands were deceased conquistadors. Both would remain in New Spain, and both "became respectable heads of households, property owners, and esteemed leaders. Their dreams of carving a place for themselves in the New World had come true."[135]

For Cabeza de Vaca, the remainder of his life would be played out in Spain and South America. And his years of trekking into regions unknown to Spaniards were far from over. He rested for two months in Mexico City and then set out for Veracruz, where he booked passage on a ship then in harbor. When he was about to embark in October 1536, a storm in the hurricane season came ashore and capsized the vessel, whereupon don Álvar sensibly decided to spend the winter in the port city.[136]

Cabeza de Vaca sailed from Veracruz on April 10, 1537. After a stopover in Cuba, he left the port of Havana on June 2. Any crossing of the Atlantic on ships of that era was perilous. Storms threatened to capsize or disable vessels on the high seas, and there was the added threat of enemy warships. This was a time of almost constant warfare between Charles V of Spain and Francis I of France, and indeed Cabeza de Vaca stressed his fears of capture by the French. He and his shipmates were fortunate to reach the safety of the Azores after twenty-nine days, having previously survived a bad storm near Bermuda.

At this time, the Spanish and Portuguese were on good terms, and from the Azores to Lisbon the Spanish vessel and its passengers welcomed the presence of any Portuguese ship. They were soon lucky to find themselves approached by a Portuguese galleon commanded by a captain with exceptionally "salty language." The captain asked the destination of the Spanish vessel and agreed to accompany it to port. In his ship-to-ship communication, Captain Diego de Silveira observed (in Portuguese), "you have a very bad ship and very bad artillery!"—followed by, "Son of bitch, there's that renegade French ship and what a good mouthful she's lost!" Silveira then added, "Follow me and don't get separated from me, for with the help of God, I'll get you to Castile."[137]

The ship bearing Cabeza de Vaca made port for Lisbon and arrived there without further incident on August 9. Whether don Álvar traveled to Spain by land or sea is unclear, but in November he informed the House of Trade in Seville that he planned to visit the royal court and seek a license to conquer and settle the vast lands previously awarded to Pánfilo de Narváez. He would soon learn, however, that even as he crossed the

Atlantic that prize had already been awarded to Hernando de Soto on April 20, 1537.[138]

Charles V's choice of Soto as captain of a new venture in Florida was logical in terms of don Hernando's leadership abilities and wealth. The king's appointee was a splendid horseman in the prime of life, and he had returned to Spain from the conquest of Peru rich in Inca gold and silver beyond most men's dreams. But Soto was also one of the most brutal Spanish conquistadors. He offered Cabeza de Vaca a position in his expedition, but the latter decided to seek appointment to another government and not serve under someone else's command. Given the fate that awaited Soto and many of his men, don Álvar would never have reason to regret his decision. Furthermore, Cabeza de Vaca knew all too well Soto's reputation for cruelty and mistreatment of Indians, which ran counter to his belief in peaceful colonization.[139]

Having declined involvement in the Soto expedition, which left Spain in April 1538, Cabeza de Vaca probably spent the next two years preparing his *Relación* for publication. In any event, during this time he was unable to gain an audience with the crown. But the continuing rivalry of Spain and France for colonial possessions in America eventually provided that opportunity. Of immediate concern to the Spanish crown was the determination of Francis I to challenge Spain's New World empire at any point of perceived weakness, and there was indeed weakness in the region of the Río de la Plata in South America.

The Spanish had founded Buenos Aires in 1535 and placed the colony under the capable leadership of Pedro de Mendoza. Indians, who quickly tired of supplying food to the Spanish outpost, launched repeated attacks. Almost constant warfare, coupled with disease and lack of food, had taken the lives of more than a thousand people in two years.[140]

In search of a better site, Mendoza sent several parties up the region's major rivers in the 1530s. One of the entradas was led by Juan de Salazar who founded the town of Asunción on the left bank of the Paraguay River, but from the beginning this outpost hung by a slender thread. Its settlers faced constant threats from Indians and suffered from the lack of food and supplies.[141]

Pedro de Mendoza, suffering from syphilis, gave up on the Buenos Aires colony in late 1539 and sailed for Spain but died at sea aboard the *Magdalena*. With Mendoza's departure, Juan de Ayolas had assumed power as lieutenant governor but soon departed to lead still another expedition to the interior in search of mines, leaving interim governor Domingo Martínez de Irala in charge. Irala, like Mendoza, thought the colony unsustainable and moved the seat of government to the small outpost at

Asunción in present-day Paraguay. There matters quickly improved under Irala's hand. The colonists liked him, enjoyed the privilege of enslaving Indians, and appreciated a governor who was "quite indifferent to all concerns of pelf."[142]

The upshot of Spain's leaving Buenos Aires almost abandoned was its attractiveness to French interests in the great estuary, which was the pathway to a region long believed to be rich in silver and was thus optimistically named the Río de la Plata (River of Silver). There was also concern at the Spanish court that mistreatment of Indians had been an important factor in the failure of the South American colony at Buenos Aires. So, why not appoint a man as governor who was skilled in Indian relations and who was also willing to invest eight thousand *ducados* in the venture?[143]

Thus, Cabeza de Vaca was finally admitted to the Spanish court, and on March 18, 1540, Charles V awarded him a contract, which included his appointments as governor and military captain of the Río de la Plata—but only if Juan de Ayolas were dead. If alive, don Álvar would be second in command as lieutenant governor. But in either case, Cabeza de Vaca received possession of Santa Catalina Island, situated off the Brazilian coastline about midway between the mouth of the Amazon and the Río de la Plata.[144] His main concern, however, would be an Atlantic crossing.

Spanish voyages to the eastern coast of South America, although far safer than sailing around the Horn to Chile and Peru, were nonetheless long and perilous undertakings in the sixteenth century. Because of distance, as well as adverse winds and currents, they occasionally took as much as three times longer than those from the Canaries to the Caribbean Islands. Due to extreme difficulties in communication between the crown and the Río de la Plata colony, settlers there had the highly unusual right to choose a governor in the event that the crown appointee died in office, or was deemed unfit to rule—all important to the future of Cabeza de Vaca.

Uncertain about the fate of Ayolas but determined to accept another governing position in the Indies where he might be fully in command as governor and military captain, Cabeza de Vaca purchased three ships and recruited about 250 settlers. All preparations were in place by late September 1540, but unfavorable winds at Cádiz delayed departure until December 2. With stops for buying a fourth ship, taking on fresh water, and making ship repairs in the Canary and Cape Verde islands, landfall on Santa Catalina came on March 29, 1541.[145] (see Figure 11)

In May, Cabeza de Vaca sent two ships toward Buenos Aires to relieve a few defenders who still manned its fort. The rescue effort failed, because strong south winds blew the vessels on shore and destroyed them. The

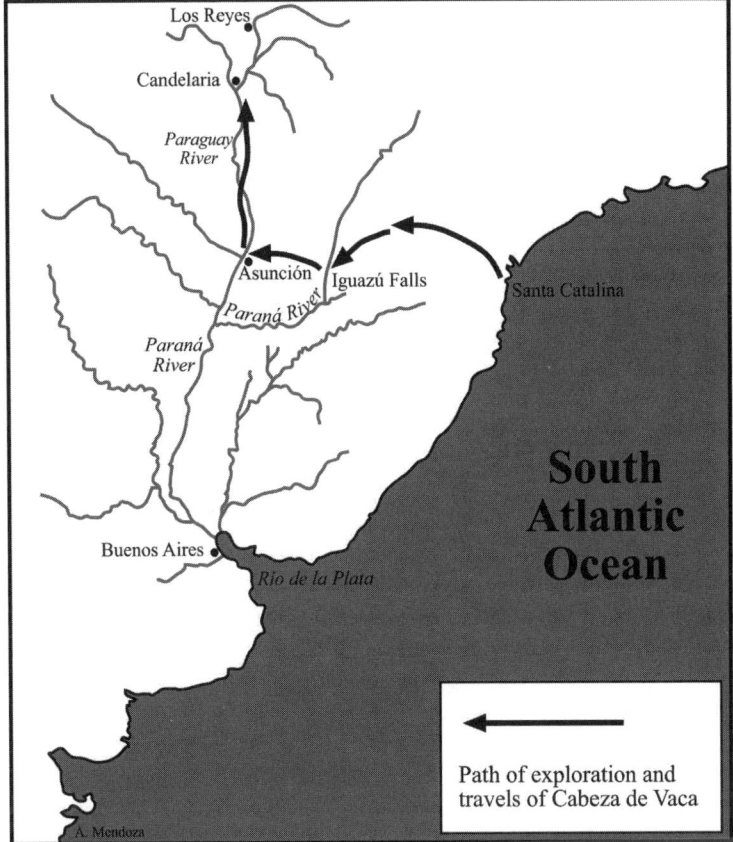

Figure 11. Path of Cabeza de Vaca's explorations and travels in South America, 1540–1544. Cartography by Alex Mendoza. After map in David A. Howard's *Conquistador in Chains*, p. 47. Copyright University of Alabama Press, 1997. Permission by Claire Lewis Evans.

wrecks, however, occurred close to Santa Catalina, and most of the crews returned safely to the island. Later in the same month, a few Spaniards in a rickety craft sailed from Buenos Aires and arrived on the island. With them came news that Juan de Ayolas was dead. He and his men had been killed by Payaguáes Indians. However sad the news, it meant that Cabeza de Vaca could rule with full titles.[146]

Given the proven difficulty of sailing south to the great estuary at Buenos Aires and beyond, where he and his company could have made a waterway entry to Asunción, Cabeza de Vaca decided to leave Santa Catalina, land on the Brazilian coast, and march to the town. His decision was met with a storm of protests. All dissenters agreed that the interior was a trackless wilderness filled with cannibals, impassable rivers, jungles, and poisonous snakes. Don Álvar calmly pointed out that he knew how to handle unknown regions and that an overland route would give him the opportunity to make peace with the Indians. Besides, as he reminded his followers, he was captain, and they would do as he ordered.[147]

On October 18, 1541, Cabeza de Vaca assembled on the coast of Brazil a company of 250 (twenty-six mounted), several wives, a few dozen Indians carriers, and two Franciscan priests. To inspire his men, he chose to take off his shoes and walk barefoot the more than 1,200 miles to Asunción![148]

The march was fraught with difficulties. The company had to traverse forests so dense that the men had to clear the way with swords, ford rivers so tortuous that they required multiple crossings, and wade marshlands so devoid of food that the only sustenance came from white worms found in the hollows of reeds. On occasion, the columns passed through villages with more than ample food, but others had not enough, which led to quarrels over its distribution. Still other problems arose from those who advocated different pathways to their destination.[149]

Cabeza de Vaca and his followers were the first Europeans of record to see the magnificent Iguazú Falls, where they arrived on January 31, 1542. The distance from the falls to Asunción still required a march of just fewer than forty-five days, and near the end Cabeza de Vaca tactfully sent notice to Domíngo de Irala of his impending arrival and assumption of power. He completed his remarkable journey by walking into Asunción on the morning of March 11, 1542.[150]

The march had taken four and a half months and resulted in amazingly few fatalities. By some accounts there was no loss of life whatsoever, but it appears that two men lost their lives—one was killed by a jaguar, the other "became sick and, helped along by an arrow, died."[151] But the amazing leadership of Cabeza de Vaca, in crossing a largely unknown land with so little loss of life, was to be the high point in his South American governorship. His troubles were about to begin, and they would plague him for the remainder of his life.

Initially, the ragged and isolated settlers at Asunción were pleased by the arrival of additional Spaniards, much-needed supplies, and the twenty-six horses, for not one of the mounts—incredible as it may seem—had died on the trek. But as historian J. H. Parry has remarked: "The gratitude of the settlers did not last long."[152]

Among Cabeza de Vaca's subjects as governor were hundreds of

Guaraní Indians. Their manners soon came to the attention of don Álvar and probably kindled reminders of his Texas experiences. Guaraní medicine men cured ills with incantations and by sucking wounds, followed by producing a pebble secreted in the mouth of the provider as "proof" of having removed the poisoning agent. the Guaranís were also cannibals who ate the flesh of their enemies, which hardly endeared them to their Spanish overlords. Cabeza de Vaca, of course, saw the natives in a much different light, and he was determined to champion their rights as fellow human beings, but he could not countenance their cannibalism.[153]

On April 5, 1542, less than a month after his arrival in Asunción, Cabeza de Vaca issued his first decree as governor, which called for the removal of unrelated Indian women from Spanish dwellings within six days. He followed this edict with a spate of laws. Included (astonishingly) were night-time curfews for rough-hewn Spaniards, guarantees of Indians' privacy and property rights, restrictions on Spaniards entering Indians' lodging without the governor's permission, prohibitions on the sale of Indian lands or homes without formal sanction, and interdicts on forcing Indians to trade items against their will.[154]

The governor's edicts, certain to cause trouble, were read by criers for the illiterate and publicly posted for those who were not. Offenders could be fined, sent to jail, placed in stocks, or forced to serve as oarsmen on Spanish vessels. His enemies at Asunción, who grew rapidly in number, countered that "his 'humane' Indian policy was aimed only at persuading the Spanish government of his innocence when he was accused of crimes."[155]

On April 29, 1542, Cabeza de Vaca followed with orders designed to curb cannibalism. The Indians were to stop eating human flesh "for the serious sin and offense that they were committing by it against God our Lord." His agents of persuasion and enforcement were his subordinates in government and the Franciscan missionaries.[156]

The willingness of Spaniards to comply with unpopular laws and those of a similar vein that followed is questionable, and in any event, they did not last long. In mid-April 1544, a mutinous cabal stormed into Cabeza de Vaca's house in Asunción. With shouts of "Liberty! Liberty!" the rebels threatened to kill don Álvar by jabbing swords and daggers at his chest. Others shouted "Tyrant" at Cabeza de Vaca and "Long live the king" as he was hauled off to jail.[157]

As historian Parry has suggested, the uprising that stripped Cabeza de Vaca of power resulted from his efforts to protect the Indians from harm, but the rebels dared not make this argument to Charles V. The king, under pressure from reformist elements in Spain, had already issued the New Laws of 1542, which were designed to correct the most serious abuses perpetrated on Indians by Spaniards.[158]

Awareness of the New Laws probably did not reach Asunción until 1544 or early 1545. At that time, the rebels began to concoct a story of don Álvar's *mistreatment* of Indians. And for good measure, they accused him of disloyalty to the king. Both charges were essentially without foundation.[159]

Cabeza de Vaca, like all human beings, was nonetheless far from perfect. With some apparent justice, his detractors pointed to don Álvar's displaying his own coat of arms, rather than the royal standard (see Figure 12). Much less likely, since testimony in Asunción was from sworn enemies, were *words* allegedly uttered by Cabeza de Vaca: "[I am] king and lord of this land." Some critics also claimed that the governor had professed to being both king and pope—words most unlikely from a devout Christian—and words, if true, that would have landed Cabeza de Vaca before a tribunal of the Spanish Inquisition. As for don Álvar's mistreatment of Indians, evidence to the contrary lies in the complete overturn of his Indian policies during his incarceration.[160]

On March 7, 1545, rebels roused Cabeza de Vaca from a cell in Asunción, where he had languished since April 15, 1544, and sent him toward the ocean. En route, his food was laced with arsenic sulfide. He averted death in the first poisoning by using an emetic of oil. In the second and third instances, he refused the meals and did not eat anything for four days. When at last he was put aboard an oceangoing ship, he spent the crossing shackled in irons.[161]

During his trial in Spain, it was exceptionally difficult for Cabeza de Vaca to mount an effective defense, primarily because he could not obtain testimony from those favorable to his actions in the colony or with supporting documentation, such as the ordinances he had issued as governor concerning the welfare and good treatment of Indians. And how could he prove loyalty to the king with so much testimony about his disloyalty as sworn by his enemies? Furthermore, the rebels in Asunción had sent two hand-picked agents to guard Cabeza de Vaca onboard ship and "to defend the rebellion before the king."[162] The verdict in his trial was a foregone conclusion.

On March 18, 1551, Cabeza de Vaca was declared guilty of all thirty-two charges against him. He was stripped of titles, banished in perpetuity on pain of death from all Spanish possessions in the Indies, and sentenced to five years' service at the penal colony of Oran in North Africa. During the ordeal of his lengthy trial from summer 1546 to the date of sentenc-

Figure 12. Coat of arms of the House of Cabeza de Vaca. Courtesy Houghton Library, Harvard University, Span 384210★.

ing, Cabeza de Vaca initially spent time in the royal jail at court, but for most of those years he was under house arrest and treated as a gentleman. He would launch petition after petition for a lessened sentence, and he was finally successful on August 23, 1552. On that date, his perpetual banishment from the Indies was limited to the jurisdiction of the Río de la Plata, and he was freed of sentence at Oran.[163]

During the next six to seven years, Cabeza de Vaca remained in Spain and spent at least part of that time preparing the second edition of his *Relación* for publication in 1555. From that time until his death c.1559, his official residence was in Jerez de la Frontera. His burial site is unknown but may have been in the family vault at the Real Convento de Santo Domingo in the town of his birth.[164]

Afterword

THE REMARKABLE TRAVELS of Álvar Núñez Cabeza de Vaca in North and South America require no analysis. They are simply amazing in themselves. He was one of only four to survive the disastrous Pánfilo de Narváez overland expedition to Florida and beyond. Don Álvar and three companions then trekked some 2,800 miles on bare feet from the Texas coast near Galveston Island to Mexico City. Later on, Cabeza de Vaca reprised that journey by walking just less than half that distance from the east coast of Brazil to the town of Asunción in modern-day Paraguay. In both instances, he traversed lands previously unknown to Europeans.

It is his transformation from proud Spanish don, second in command in the Narváez expedition, to lay advocate of Indian rights on both American continents that requires careful consideration. That journey is almost as remarkable as his travels.

What was it that set Cabeza de Vaca apart from thousands of fellow Spaniards in his advocacy of Indian rights as a secular person? Unfortunately, there is no clear answer to this question. Yes, he was better educated than many conquistadors and settlers in the Americas, as evidenced by his writing in two editions of his *Relación*, and he probably could out think many others. And, yes, he was awarded positions of importance and command in two expeditions on two continents. But this still begs the question.

Very few individuals in history dramatically transcend contemporaries with similar backgrounds, goals, and values. For example, Bartolomé de las Casas began his career as an *encomendero* (possessor of an encomienda) on the island of Española. He was just as exploitive of Indians as fellow encomenderos until something life-altering struck him in 1514.[165] He gave up his encomienda, returned to Spain in 1515, entered the Dominican Order, and spent the next fifty years as the most passionate advocate of Indian rights in the Spanish Indies.

Something similar to the "great awakening" experienced by Las Casas happened with Cabeza de Vaca, despite his having endured months of threats, mistreatment, beatings, and enslavement by Coahuiltecans in Texas. His two Spanish companions, Alonso del Castillo and Andrés Dorantes, had essentially identical experiences in Texas. Yet both, when the opportunity presented itself in 1536, married wealthy widows and became encomenderos in Mexico. Again, why did Cabeza de Vaca follow a radically different path than that of his former companions?

Cabeza de Vaca was more ambitious than they, and he desired a governmental position where he had the authority to institute his ideas centered on better treatment for Indians. He was aware of Hernando de Soto's brutal instincts and demurred serving under his command in 1539. Three years later, he seized the opportunity to head the government in Asunción as governor and military commander.

Converts to a cause, whatever it might be, are often not easy to like. They have "seen" what is "right" and are doggedly determined that everyone else see things their way. Converts are usually contrary and incapable of compromise, as well as unlikely to discern or even care just how unpopular they are with others of a different mind-set.

In one of the poorest, most remote, and benighted areas of the Spanish empire, where Domingo de Irala had allowed free rein to settlers at Asunción, Cabeza de Vaca metaphorically tried to turn the tide with edicts and ordinances on behalf of Indians. He would have been wise to have adopted the governing philosophy of Antonio de Mendoza, the first viceroy of New Spain, whom he met in 1536. Mendoza shrewdly observed that the proper course for a Spanish administrator in the Indies was to do little and do it slowly. For example, when the New Laws of 1542 reached Mexico in 1544, Mendoza thought that enforcement of them might well bring rebellion from settlers who possessed encomiendas. He invoked four famous words used by officials in Spanish Colonial Administration: "Obedezco pero no cumplo"—"I obey but do not comply." Mendoza bowed to the *authority* of the royal ordinances but did not immediately comply with the New Laws. He instead petitioned the crown through his agents for revision of the laws, which eventually occurred.[166]

By contrast, Blasco Núñez Vela, the first viceroy of Peru, was an obstinate martinet who carried the New Laws into the newly created viceroyalty in 1544 and insisted on immediate implementation of them. Núñez Vela's unyielding arrogance and stubbornness touched off a series of bloody civil wars in Peru that resulted in his death on January 18, 1546, following the battle of Añaquito. Wounded and perhaps dying from a blow to his head by a battle ax, the viceroy was beheaded with a saber.[167]

These events in Peru were contemporaneous with Cabeza de Vaca's governorship at Asunción, and don Álvar was lucky to have escaped with his life. It was one thing for him to have been "right" and espouse the most praiseworthy of motives for Indians—it was quite another for don Álvar to have been blind to the conditions that surrounded him. In the nineteenth century, historian William H. Prescott penned words describing what led to the death of Blasco Núñez Vela that seem applicable to Cabeza de Vaca's ill-advised polices in Paraguay. Persons in positions of authority should never enforce a law, "which circumstances show must certainly defeat the object for which it was designed. . . . But it requires sagacity to determine the existence of such a contingency, and moral courage to assume the responsibility of acting on it. Such . . . is the severest test of character."[168] Cabeza de Vaca was assuredly a good man but did not understand the limits of his authority or the temper of the Paraguayan colonists. Nonetheless, it is a supreme irony that he was tried and convicted on trumped-up charges for carrying out policies that were the exact opposite of what he had promoted—the humane protection of Indians at Asunción.

Notes to Introduction
1. Donald E. Chipman, "In Search of Cabeza de Vaca's Route across Texas: An Historiographical Survey," *Southwestern Historical Quarterly* 91 (October 1987): 144.
2. Santa Catalina Island was renamed Santa Catarina when it became a part of Brazil.
3. David A. Howard, *Conquistador in Chains: Cabeza de Vaca and the Indians of the Americas* (Tuscaloosa: University of Alabama Press, 1997), 51.
4. Ibid., 56.

Notes to Chapter One
5. Readers wishing to pursue the origins of the Martín de Alhaja legend are referred to Rolena Adorno and Patrick Charles Pautz, *Álvar Núñez Cabeza de Vaca: His Accounts, His Life, and the Expedition of Pánfilo de Narváez* (3 vols.; Lincoln: University of Nebraska Press, 1999), 1: 301–305.
6. Ibid., 306–315.
7. Ibid., 343.
8. Ibid., 325–330 (quotation on 325).
9. Ibid., 330–331.
10. Ibid., 314–315, Table 2.
11. Ibid., 324, table. See idem, 343, for names of Cabeza de Vaca's younger brothers.
12. Ibid., 360.
13. Ibid., 359.
14. Ibid., 359–360, 366–369.
15. J. H. Elliott, *Imperial Spain, 1469–1716* (New York: St. Martin Press, 1964), 141–149.
16. Donald E. Chipman and Harriett Denise Joseph, *Spanish Texas, 1519–1821* (rev. ed.; Austin: University of Texas Press, 2010), 24.
17. Ibid.
18. Ibid., 27. The Veracruz mentioned in this paragraph was not the port city as we know it today; instead it refers to Villa Rica de la Veracruz, located some thirty-five miles up the coast from present-day Veracruz, which was settled at its current site in 1599.
19. Donald E. Chipman, *Moctezuma's Children: Aztec Royalty under Spanish Rule, 1520–1700* (Austin: University of Texas Press, 2005), 36.
20. Chipman and Joseph, *Spanish Texas*, 27; Andrés Reséndez, *A Land So Strange: The Epic Journey of Cabeza de Vaca* (New York: Basic Books, 2007), 43.
21. Adorno and Pautz, *Cabeza de Vaca*, 1: 372.
22. Reséndez, *A Land So Strange*, 43, as quoted.
23. Adorno and Pautz, *Cabeza de Vaca*, 1: 373.
24. Reséndez, *A Land So Strange*, 44–45.
25. Ibid., 46–47.
26. Adorno and Pautz, *Cabeza de Vaca*, 2: 45–47.
27. Ibid., 47, as quoted. On one of the islands, Narváez purchased a sixth ship.
28. Reséndez, *A Land So Strange*, 64–66.
29. Adorno and Pautz, *Cabeza de Vaca*, 2: 29.
30. Ibid.
31. Ibid., 31.
32. Ibid.; Adorno and Pautz, *Cabeza de Vaca*, 1: 37n.4. The full name of the pilot was likely Diego Fernández de Miruelo.
33. Reséndez, *A Land So Strange*, 83–84.
34. Chipman and Joseph, *Spanish Texas*, 24–28.

Notes to Chapter Two

35. Reséndez, *A Land So Strange*, 84.
36. Adorno and Pautz, *Cabeza de Vaca*, 1: 35.
37. Reséndez, *A Land So Strange*, 85–86.
38. Ibid., 86.
39. Ibid.
40. Chipman and Joseph, *Spanish Texas*, 44.
41. Reséndez, *A Land So Strange*, 86–88 (quotation on 86–87).
42. Adorno and Pautz, *Cabeza de Vaca*, 1: 45.
43. Reséndez, *A Land So Strange*, 89.
44. Ibid., 106–109
45. Enrique Pupo-Walker (ed.), and Frances M. López-Morillas (trans.), *Castaways: The Narrative of Alvar Núñez Cabeza de Vaca* (Berkeley: University of California Press, 1993), 17.
46. Reséndez, *A Land So Strange*, 94–95. Cabeza de Vaca did make one foray to the coast to search for the ships but found only shallows and oyster reefs.
47. Adorno and Pautz, *Cabeza de Vaca*, 1: 55.
48. Reséndez, *A Land So Strange*, 96–104 (brief quotation on 98).
49. Ibid., 105–106 (1st quotation on 105); Adorno and Pautz, *Cabeza de Vaca*, 1: 67, 69 (2nd quotation).
50. Chipman and Joseph, *Spanish Texas*, 29.
51. Reséndez, *A Land So Strange*, 115–119.
52. Adorno and Pautz, *Cabeza de Vaca*, 1: 75 (1st quotation); 77 (2nd quotation).
53. Ibid., 81.
54. Ibid., 81, 83 (quotation on 83).
55. Ibid., 85, 87.
56. Ibid., 87, 89 (quotation on 87).
57. Ibid., 89.
58. Ibid., 89 (1st quotation); 91 (2nd quotation).
59. Ibid., 91.
60. Ibid., 91 (1st and 2nd quotations); 93 (3rd and 4th quotations).

Notes to Chapter Three

61. Chipman, "In Search of Cabeza de Vaca's Route across Texas," 127–148.
62. Adorno and Pautz, *Cabeza de Vaca*, 1: 95.
63. Ibid., 99.
64. Ibid., 101.
65. Chipman and Joseph, *Spanish Texas*, 30; Matthew S. Taylor, "Cabeza de Vaca and the Introduction of Disease to Texas," *Southwestern Historical Quarterly* 111 (April 2008): 420–421, 426, quotation. For evidence of pre-Columbian hemorrhagic fevers in bones of Indians at nearby sites, see Taylor, 426–427.
66. Reséndez, *A Land So Strange*, map on 129, 2nd quotation on 131; Adorno and Pautz, *Cabeza de Vaca*, 1: 133 (1st quotation).
67. Adorno and Pautz, *Cabeza de Vaca*, 1: 123.
68. Ibid., 109.
69. Ibid., 113.
70. Ibid., 115.
71. Ibid., 121. By going forward, Cabeza de Vaca meant toward the Río de las Palmas.
72. Chipman, "In Search of Cabeza de Vaca's Route across Texas," 133.
73. Adorno and Pautz, *Cabeza de Vaca*, 1: 123.

74. Ibid., 125.

75. Ibid., 127.

76. Ibid., 129.

Notes to Chapter Four

77. Chipman and Joseph, *Spanish Texas*, 16, quotations as quoted. Excellent information on early Coahuiltecan people may also be found in Robert S. Weddle, *San Juan Bautista: Gateway to Spanish Texas* (Austin: University of Texas Press, 1968) and in Isidro Félix de Espinosa, *Crónica de los Colegios de Propaganda Fide de la Nueva España* (Washington, D.C.: Academy of American Franciscan History, 1964).

78. T. N. Campbell and T. J. Campbell, *Historic Indian Groups of the Choke Canyon Reservoir and Surrounding Area, Southern Texas* (San Antonio: Center for Archaeological Research, 1981), 10–11.

79. Ibid., 7.

80. Chipman and Joseph, *Spanish Texas*, 17.

81. Ibid.

82. W. W. Newcomb Jr., forward, in T. N. Campbell, *The Indians of Southern Texas and Northeastern Mexico: Selected Writings of Thomas Nolan Campbell* (Austin: Texas Archeological Research Laboratory, 1990), ix.

83. Reséndez, *A Land So Strange*, 160; Adorno and Pautz, *Cabeza de Vaca*, 1: 147.

84. Adorno and Pautz, *Cabeza de Vaca*, 1: 143. Areitos would later be suppressed as pagan rituals by Spanish church and government officials.

85. Ibid., 143, 145, quotations on both pages.

86. Ibid., 147.

87. Donald E. Chipman and Harriett Denise Joseph, *Notable Men and Women of Spanish Texas* (Austin: University of Texas Press, 1999), 11.

88. Ibid., as quoted.

89. Reséndez, *A Land So Strange*, 165.

90. Ibid., 164–166.

91. Pupo-Walker and López-Morillas, *Castaways*, 66.

92. Ibid., 66–67.

93. Adorno and Pautz, *Cabeza de Vaca*, 1: 155.

94. Ibid.

95. Ibid.

96. Ibid., 157, 159 (quotation on 159).

97. Ibid., 161.

98. Alex D. Krieger, *We Came Naked and Barefoot: The Journey of Cabeza de Vaca across North America*, ed. Margery H. Krieger (Austin: University of Texas Press, 2002), 202.

99. Adorno and Pautz, *Cabeza de Vaca*, 1: 165.

100. Ibid., 167.

101. Ibid. (1st quotation); 169 (2nd quotation).

Notes to Chapter Five

102. Reséndez, *A Land So Strange*, 177.

103. Ibid.

104. Adorno and Pautz, *Cabeza de Vaca*, 2: 418–419.

105. Reséndez, *A Land So Strange*, 179.

106. Adorno and Pautz, *Cabeza de Vaca*, 1: 171–173 (1st quotation); 173 (2nd quotation).

107. Ibid., 173.

108. Ibid., 181. As mentioned in Chapter 1, Cabeza de Vaca had fought in Italy at the Battle of Ravenna in 1512.

109. Thomas R. Hester, foreword, in Krieger, *We Came Naked and Barefoot*, xi; see also T. N. Campbell, *The Indians of Southern Texas*. For advocacy of a trans-Texas route, see Nancy P. Hickerson, *The Jumanos: Hunters and Traders of the South Plains* (Austin: University of Texas Press, 1994), 7–18.

110. Chipman, "In Search of Cabeza de Vaca's Route across Texas," 145–146.

111. Adorno and Pautz, *Cabeza de Vaca*, 1: 209.

112. See Jesse E. Thompson, "Sagittectomy—First Recorded Surgical Procedure in the American Southwest, 1535: The Journey and Ministrations of Álvar Núñez Cabeza de Vaca," *New England Journal of Medicine* 289 (December 27, 1973): 1403–1407.

113. Campbell and Campbell, *Historic Indian Groups*, 9.

114. For characteristics of *Pinus remota* and information on its extremely limited range, see Donald W. Olson et al., "Piñon Pines and the Route of Cabeza de Vaca," *Southwestern Historical Quarterly* 101 (October 1997): 174–186.

115. Reséndez, *A Land So Strange*, 190–191 (quotation on 190).

116. Herbert E. Bolton (ed.), *Spanish Exploration in the Southwest, 1542–1706* (Reprint, New York: Barnes and Noble, 1963), 173; Chipman and Joseph, *Spanish Texas*, 54. The expedition's leader was Antonio de Espejo, who arrived at the Indian settlement in late 1582.

117. Adorno and Pautz, *Cabeza de Vaca*, 1: 221.

118. Chipman, "In Search of Cabeza de Vaca's Route across Texas," 146.

119. Reséndez, *A Land So Strange*, 202.

120. Adorno and Pautz, *Cabeza de Vaca*, 1: 231.

121. Ibid., 239.

122. Ibid., 245 (quotation); Chipman and Joseph, *Spanish Texas*, 34.

123. Adorno and Pautz, *Cabeza de Vaca*, 1: 247, n.3.

124. Ibid., 251.

125. Reséndez, *A Land So Strange*, 209.

Notes to Chapter Six

126. Reséndez, *A Land So Strange*, 212–213.

127. Ibid., 214.

128. Adorno and Pautz, *Cabeza de Vaca*, 1: 265; Reséndez, *A Land So Strange*, 215.

129. Adorno and Pautz, *Cabeza de Vaca*, 1: 265; David A. Howard, *Conquistador in Chains: Cabeza de Vaca and the Indians of the Americas* (Tuscaloosa: University of Alabama Press, 1997), 30.

130. Adorno and Pautz, *Cabeza de Vaca*, 1: 265 and ns.7, 8.

131. Reséndez, *A Land So Strange*, 224–226 (quotation on 226).

132. Chipman and Joseph, *Spanish Texas*, 31.

133. See Gonzalo Fernández de Oviedo, *Historia general y natural de las Indias* (5 vols.; Madrid: Ediciones Atlas, 1959), 4: 287–318; for the best translation of the Joint Report, see Basil C. Hedrick and Carroll L. Riley, *The Journey of the Vaca Party: The Account of the Narváez Expedition, 1528–1536* (Carbondale: Southern Illinois University Press, 1974).

134. The recollections of Castillo and Dorantes during their years of separation from Cabeza de Vaca (1529–1532) are valuable for documenting instances of cannibalism among desperately hungry Spaniards and the murder of others by coastal Indians.

135. Reséndez, *A Land So Strange*, 222–224 (quotation on 224). Dorantes initially sailed for Spain in 1537, but when the vessel took on water and had to return to port, he chose not to risk a second Atlantic crossing.

136. Adorno and Pautz, *Cabeza de Vaca*, 1: 265, 267. As a reminder, the Veracruz mentioned here was Villa Rica de la Veracruz, some thirty-five miles up the coast from the modern port city and the fortress of San Juan de Ulúa.

137. Ibid., 271. The profanity in Portuguese was "*Ó fi de puta!*"

138. Howard, *Conquistador in Chains*, 31–33.

139. Ibid., 33–34.

140. Ibid., 38.

141. J. H. Parry, *The Discovery of South America* (New York: Taplinger Publishing Compay, 1979), 254.

142. Ibid.; Howard, *Conquistador in Chains*, 38–39; R. B. Cunningham Graham, *The Conquest of the River Plate* (New York: Doubleday, 1924), 86 (quotation). Buenos Aires was not totally abandoned. A few stalwarts continued to hold out at its fort. The site was finally abandoned in 1541.

143. Howard, *Conquistador in Chains*, 39–40.

144. "Capitulación que se tomó con Álvar Núñez Cabeza de Vaca, 1540," *Colección de documentos inéditos relativos al descubrimiento, conquista y organización de las antiguas posesiones de América y Oceanía* (42 vols; Madrid: Kraus Reprint, 1966), 23: 8–33.

145. Howard, *Conquistador in Chains*, 45.

146. Ibid., 47–47; Morris Bishop, *The Odyssey of Cabeza de Vaca* (New York: Century Company, 1933), 195. See n.140 above.

147. Bishop, *Odyssey*, 196–197.

148. Ibid., 198.

149. Howard, *Conquistador in Chains*, 54–57.

150. Ibid., 56–63; Parry, *Discovery*, 254.

151. Howard, *Conquistador in Chains*, 63.

152. Parry, *Discovery*, 257. Irala was confirmed as governor of the Río de la Plata by Charles V in 1552 and remained in control until his death in 1556.

153. Bishop, *Odyssey*, 205–207.

154. Howard, *Conquistador in Chains*, 71.

155. Ibid., 71–72, quotation on 72.

156. Ibid., 74–75, quotation, as quoted, on 74.

157. Ibid., 147.

158. For the New Laws' provisions, see Lewis Hanke, *The Spanish Struggle for Justice in the Conquest of the Americas* (Dallas: Southern Methodist University Press, 2002), 91–92, or access <http://www.fordham.edu/halsall/mod/1542newlawsindies.html>; see also Howard, *Conquistador in Chains*, 187.

159. Howard, *Conquistador in Chains*, 155.

160. Ibid., 155–161 (quotation on 158).

161. Ibid., 185–186.

162. Ibid., 171.

163. Adorno and Pautz, *Cabeza de Vaca*, 1: 398–400.

164. Ibid., 407–412. In these pages, Adorno and Pautz effectively lay to rest the assertion of some authors that Cabeza de Vaca died in poverty.

Afterword

165. Hanke, *The Spanish Struggle for Justice*, 56. *Encomienda* is an enormously complicated institution impossible to describe fully in a few words. In its simplest form, it involved the assigning of free Indian vassals (not slaves) in a specific locale to a Spanish overseer (*encomendero*). The Indians had work or tribute obligations to their overlord, who *in theory* was

to protect his charges and ensure their conversion to Christianity. A grant of *encomienda* did not include the Indians' land. For a thorough understanding of the institution, see Silvio A. Zavala, *La encomienda indiana* (Madrid: Librería de E. Prieto, 1936).

166. Chipman, *Moctezuma's Children*, 86–87.

167. James M. Lockhart, *Spanish Peru, 1532–1560: A Colonial Society* (Madison: University of Wisconsin Press), 4–5; William H. Prescott, *History of the Conquest of Mexico and History of the Conquest of Peru* (New York: Modern Library, [1936]), 1153.

168. Prescott, *History of the Conquest of Peru*, 1154–1155.

INDEX